The Computer Culture

The Computer Culture

A Symposium to Explore the Computer's Impact on Society

Edited by
Denis P. Donnelly

Rutherford • Madison • Teaneck
Fairleigh Dickinson University Press
London and Toronto: Associated University Presses

Associated University Presses
440 Forsgate Drive
Cranbury, NJ 08512

Associated University Presses
25 Sicilian Avenue
London WC1A 2QH, England

Associated University Presses
2133 Royal Windsor Drive
Unit 1
Mississauga, Ontario
Canada L5J 1K5

Library of Congress Cataloging in Publication Data
Main entry under title:

The Computer culture.

Edited proceedings of the Computer Culture Symposium.
Bibliography: p.
1. Computers—Social aspects—Congresses. I. Donnelly, Denis P., 1937– . II. Computer Culture Symposium (1981: Siena College)
QA76.9.C66C634 1985 303.4′834 83-49215
ISBN 0-8386-3220-3

Figures 6, 7, and 8 are reproduced from *World Dynamics*, 2d ed. (1973) with the kind permission of Professor Jay W. Forrester and the M.I.T. Press.

Printed in the United States of America

for Walter and Dorothy

Contents

Notes on Contributors

DAVID F. ANDERSEN is the dean of the Graduate School of Public Affairs, State University of New York at Albany (SUNY). He came to SUNY in 1977 after completing his graduate work at the Massachusetts Institute of Technology. He still teaches system dynamics and social policy design in the Department of Public Administration.

DENIS P. DONNELLY received his Ph.D. in nuclear physics from the University of Michigan. He is the author of a number of papers on nuclear physics, atomic beams, electronic instrumentation, and scientific pedagogy. He holds a patent for a meteorological device. At present Dr. Donnelly is dean of the Division of Science at Siena College.

WARREN HOCKENOS is a member of the Department of Philosophy at Skidmore College. A graduate of Boston University, he teaches courses in logic and the philosophy of science. His particular areas of interest include the philosophy of language and ethology.

MARVIN MINSKY, Donner Professor of Science at Massachusetts Institute of Technology, is noted for his work in artificial intelligence. He is a member of the National Academy of Science and a fellow of the Harvard Society of Fellows, the Institute of Electrical and Electronics Engineers, and the American Academy of Arts and Sciences.

BERTON D. MOLDOW has been a member of International Business Machine Corporation's System Research Institute since 1977. A graduate of City College of New York and George Washington University, he teaches courses related to the design, development, and marketing of information systems.

ROGER C. SCHANK, at Yale University since 1976, is chairman of the computer science department, director of the Yale Artificial Intelligence Program, and director of the Cognitive Science Program. He is editor of the journal *Cognitive Science* and serves on the board of editors of numerous other professional journals.

EUGENE B. SKOLNIKOFF, chairman of the Department of Political Science at Massachusetts Institute of Technology from 1970–1974, became director of the Center for International Studies at Massachusetts Institute of Technology in 1972. A Rhodes scholar and chairman of the Board of Trustees of the German Marshall Fund of the United States, he served as senior consultant to the White House Office of Science and Technology Policy.

ALAN F. WESTIN is a member of the Department of Public Law and Government at Columbia University. The author/editor of twenty books treating the impact of technology and social change on organizations, citizens, and society, he has served as a consultant in privacy to a wide range of organizations and has given expert testimony before the major committees of the United States Congress.

Preface

Every significant technological development invariably alters the culture that adopts it. Those choosing to make use of a new development have at their disposal power and control to a different degree than they had previously. These transforming capabilities often result from a change in rate, that is, the speed with which a process can be carried out, and when the increased speed—or rate—is large enough or distinctive enough, its influence can be extraordinary. Such changes range from those directly within our experience—as the ability to fell a sequoia in hours instead of days (the chainsaw vs. the ax) to those outside our experience but sufficiently dramatic to gain attention from the media—as the ability to deliver more energy in some particular location at a given time (the hydrogen bomb vs. TNT) to the subtle technological change that remains unnoticed by the layman until it becomes "worthy" of popular coverage—as the ability to increase the rate at which a switch operates (a high-speed transistor vs. the relay).

Such changes involve more than minor perturbations of the status quo. When changes effect quantitative displacements, they also become agents of qualitative change in a given environment whether one is logging in a forest or waging war on a battlefield, for example. If adopting the new process changes the fundamental rates of existing dynamic patterns of a society, the social infrastructure of the culture is altered.

Each one of the processes mentioned is part of a complex dynamic system in which each system's component responds to the states of many other components, and, in turn, each component influences a number of others. Generally, there exists a kind of dynamic equilibrium between the various elements. Significantly altering one dynamic link in the pattern produces a new dynamic balance for the whole system. For example, if the introduction of the chainsaw means that a logger can cut down trees at ten times the old rate, then the entire logging operation is affected, and everything dealing with the economics and the ecology must surely change. An accelerated wood-cutting program affects the local employment situation, the forest's ecosystem, and market dynamics. In turn, each of these changes affects many other elements (e.g., the production of wood stoves, air pollution, the cost of fire insurance). Replacing an older switch—a clacking relay, for example, such as one might find by the hundred in an older telephone switching system—with a high-speed transistor, a small, fast, efficient switch, seems at first less radical. But it is not. The potential associated with the change extends far beyond mere substitution. Transistor use means not only that certain operations can be carried out more rapidly but also that possibilities only contemplated previously have become realizable.

The implications of the transistor are still neither fully realized nor fully appreciated. The logic, architecture, and languages that have been developed are all practicable because of control over a microscopic interface, a junction between dissimilar materials. The power of the transistor switch is so far-reaching that even our concepts of mind and of the nature of intelligence have been influenced. Since the computer is a machine whose applications can be of great generality (that is, the computer can be programmed to handle a surprising variety of tasks), the introduction of this machine has exposed the links of many dynamic patterns to rapid and potentially destabilizing changes. Not only can the computer perform its operations at a prodigious rate, but unlike most technological changes that affect only one or a small set of links, the computer affects the entire spectrum of interrelationships within our culture. Any application whose operations can be put into machine code becomes subject to such a change.

The Computer Culture Symposium (1981), part of Siena College's integrated humanities program, was organized to consider the computer's present role in our culture. The program was divided into two categories: artificial intelligence (AI) and computer influences in the sociopolitical realm. This collection consists of six essays and three question-and-answer sessions—edited versions of the lectures and discussions that took place at the symposium—with the addition of a postscript.

Marvin Minsky's keynote address presents an intriguing view of the AI field while discussing the ultimate capabilities of a computer. He asks and answers questions dealing with the relationship between a computer and such features as meaning, self-awareness, creativity, consciousness, common sense, and intelligence.

Roger Schank's essay deals with a formidable problem in AI, the problem of natural language. His paper makes one aware of a number of philosophical problems as well as practical difficulties that AI researchers have encountered in their attempts to deal with natural language. His discussion provides a clear overview of the approach he has taken in dealing with the computerization of natural language.

Regrettably, the presentation on "Intelligent Systems: An Industrial Research View" by J. Gibbons of the Integrated Design/Assembly Program, General Electric Co., could not be included here because of its especially strong visual component. The lecture included some hundred slides and a brief film showing aspects of robotics-related research being performed in General Electric laboratories.

With David Andersen's paper on models, simulation, and system dynamics, attention shifts to sociopolitical concerns, the second category of the symposium. His essay deals with problems of social design. The associated discussion underscores the difficulty of incorporating assumptions into models and of interpreting output when the model is so complex that it is humanly impossible to verify the results of calculations in desired detail.

Shifting from social design, Berton Moldow discusses the marriage of computer and communications in the corporate setting. Although AI futurists may envision machine-to-machine communication with people idly standing by while computers discuss important matters not readily accessible to mortal ears, in industry the real communication problem involves people communicating with people. The industrial setting has its own goals, time horizon, and cost structure. Speculations on future computer capabilities may be fascinating, but industry must be concerned with making a profit. Industrial decisions must be made now, using the most productive combination of resources (here, computers and communication systems) currently available.

Eugene Skolnikoff shows that the problems of strategic stability extend far beyond questions of weaponry. The intricate web of interconnectedness between natural resources, communications, decision making, and equipment reliability that he describes indicates the extent and difficulty of the control problem.

In the symposium's closing paper, Alan Westin examines the problems of privacy and regulation by selecting examples from recent American history. He distinguishes between American and European approaches to regulation and confronts the nagging problem of information control, focusing on those characteristics specifically associated with the computer.

The postscript by Warren Hockenos provides a philosophical overview to one of the more perplexing problems of AI, natural language.

Special thanks are due Professor Carl Weis, coordinator, and other faculty members of the Integrated Humanities Program for their assistance, support, and cooperation in all phases of the work associated with the symposium. Professor Leon Halpert is thanked for his help in preparing part of the annotated bibliography. I especially wish to acknowledge Fr. John C. Murphy, Vice President for Academic Affairs, for his overall support of the Integrated Humanities Program, the conference, and the preparation of this work. Many thanks, too, are due Katharine Turok, managing editor of Associated University Presses, for her careful and skilled editorial assistance in preparing this work for publication.

Funding for the symposium was provided in part by a grant from the National Endowment for the Humanities. The New York Council for the Humanities generously provided funds for recording the symposium. Tapes of the original lectures as well as the question-and-answer sessions are available through interlibrary loan.

Introduction

In 1869, when Crookes and others were studying cathode rays, the future of such an enterprise was shrouded in the dark spaces that were ultimately to bear his name. Who would have guessed this was the beginning of a new technology that was to alter all but the most primitive of cultures on this earth? Who would have dreamed that the particles, the namesake of electronics, streaming through that partially evacuated tube, had properties that would seem to defy logic?

J. J. Thomson won the 1906 Nobel Prize in physics for his careful study of these rays. His work made it clear that cathode rays (now known as electrons) were subatomic *particles*. In 1937 his son, George Paget Thomson, won the Nobel Prize for his experiments involving the diffraction of electrons by crystals. His work demonstrated the *wave* nature of the same entity. The control of electrons moving through space and concomitantly the power associated with that control was achieved by treating the electron as if it were a "classical" particle. Lee De Forest's triode (1906), a primary example of such control, is a milestone in the history of electronics. The fruitfulness of the vacuum tube was immediate and long lasting.

However, since electron tubes rely on spatial control of electrons, there are fundamental limits on the design. In particular, there is a practical lower limit on size and a limit on the complexity of any one device. In the transistor, the solid state analog of the electron tube, control is no longer across space but across a junction between dissimilar materials. Thus, transistors could be reduced greatly in size, and transistor systems could be created with greatly increased complexity. But before these modern marvels were available, the computer pioneers, electrical engineers and physicists, struggled with relays and tubes to create the early computing machines.

Like the first triodes, which from our vantage point appear so crude, the initial steps toward realizing the digital computer seem equally clumsy. If the fairy tales have computer analogues, then the relay—that most inelegant and unattractive electronic device—must be the frog prince.

The principal difference is that in the computer version of the tale, the enchantment was considerably more severe: One kiss was not enough. It took years before the desired transformation occurred, and the prince emerged bedizened with silicon chips.

Before the silicon era, using designs based on relays, George Stibitz and Howard Aiken worked through the early developments of electronic computation (1937). Stibitz demonstrated the remote operation of his relay-calculating machine in 1940. Aiken's work led to the Mark I, a relay machine, which became operational in 1944. John Mauchly and J. Presper Eckert were working, too, on the development of a different system based on a tube design. The resulting machine—the electronic numerical integrator and computer (ENIAC), the first widely used electronic digital computer—became operational in 1946.

Forty years elapsed between the invention of the triode and the introduction of the ENIAC. While this machine marked a turning point in computer development, the inherent limitation of its basic structural element, the vaccum tube, doomed this machine's reliability and future development. No refinements in the tube's design could remove the limitations of this powerful classic device. At about the same time that the ENIAC, an 18,000-tube machine, was becoming fully operational, Shockley proposed an idea for a semiconductor amplifier. Not long thereafter, Bardeen and Brattain created the point-contact transistor; the following year, Shockley invented the junction transistor. By 1958, the transistor was commerically available, and the era of the electron tube was drawing to an end.

The development of integrated circuits that began in the fifties continues today with striking refinements. The number of gates on a chip has steadily increased from tens to hundreds, thousands, ten thousands, and hundred thousands. In the area of large-scale integrated circuits, Intel Corporation recently announced the 432, called the micromainframe, which includes almost 250,000 gates on three chips. Two of the chips make up the 32-bit central processing unit (CPU), while the third serves as a processor that links the 432 to other computing devices. Hewlett Packard Corporation has recently announced the development of a 32-bit single-chip CPU containing 450,000 transistors. The electronic capability of the ENIAC, which required a large room to house, is now easily exceeded by one chip.

What is the electronic capability of a computer? The crudest description of the hardware yields electronic circuits in one of two states, logic zero or logic one. What can be done at this level? Seemingly not much: the logical operations AND, OR, and NOT, or, for example, copying the contents of one location and transferring it to another. While this may sound rather limited, to gain perspective one might ask the same kind of question about a biological system. What can be done at the most fundamental level in biology? Admittedly, the systems are different; still, a crude description of DNA yields bases in essentially one of four states, A, C, T, or G. This information, too, can be copied from one location to another. One does not need to know many details of molecular biology to appreciate the relationship between DNA and a living being. It is now within present research capabilities to determine the complete code of the human genome. This example should prevent us from minimizing the potential of computer code. The limitation is not in the number of logical states at the fundamental level; the limitation is in the information contained in the code. The instructions and their implementation make the machine behave, of course, within a set of boundary conditions imposed by the limits of the machine, whether that machine be a living organism or a computer.

If one examines the operation at the opposite end of the hierarchy, where a human can most effectively interact with the computer, one finds a general-purpose machine. If one deals with numerical problems, the computer acts as a number cruncher; if one deals with symbolic problems, the machine acts as a symbol manipulator. As such, the computer must be viewed, at the least, as a tool used to extend the human capabilities of language and thought. As machines grow in complexity and overall capability, the functionality of the machine can no longer be viewed as simply a tool but must be regarded as an actual extension of man's hitherto unique symbol-manipulating capabilities. This aspect of the problem may stimulate still further discussion of what it is to be human.

Consideration of these growing computer capabilities—both their current exploitation and their future impact—provides the underlying theme of these chapters. Artificial intelligence and the sociopolitical arena comprise two distinct but related realms explored in this volume. The authors unfold their maps of the territory into which the computer's influence is inexorably expanding, and they chart the computer's path in modern culture.

The Computer Culture

Part 1
Artificial Intelligence

The elementary geometrical definitions of a straight line—the shortest distance between two points—or of a circle—the locus of points equally distant from a center—shine with a marvelous clarity. These definitions express idealizations that render a precise demarcation of zones; the edges are exact. In nature, however, there are no truly distinct edges. What may appear from afar as sharp and distinct, and as dividing two zones, at close range is seen to be irregular. At the atomic or subatomic scale, there are no sharp edges in the classical sense. At this level, simultaneous wave and particle properties of a given entity prevent such a description.

In nature, despite apparent distinctions in such characteristics as male/female (e.g., expressed in terms of hormonal milieu), essential features may, under some circumstances, become indistinguishable by any sensible criteria. The distinction between life and nonlife, which seems so clear to the naïve observer, is a complex problem when one approaches the interface of origin or the transition to nonlife. There are many criteria that one could specify to distinguish human life—for example, from a 150-pound quantity of organic fertilizer encased in the skin of a paper sack. Yet the living are sometimes transformed to the nonliving in a very gradual way. Death is a matter of a series of failures. The moment of death is not precise. Electrical activity in the brain may cease for a period sufficient for brain death to be declared, yet the patient may survive. The edges are not always clear.

Similar problems arise even within such scientific classification schemes as taxonomy. Species, as the name would seem to imply, are specific; one is, for example, a member of the species *Homo sapiens* or one is not. Our biological inheritance sets us apart. Of course, if we follow that inheritance backward in time or look at an evolutionary tree that spans the last billion years or so as a family tree, such concepts as differences between species or the concept of siblings suffer a loss of specificity. Still, of all the species, only the human being has a significant nonbiological inheritance. Of all existing species, only the human being has culture. It is highly doubtful, despite the complexity and potential information-carrying capacity of their song, that humpback whales are, like Orpheus, recounting the myths of ancient whaledom. The whales sing lyrics of the moment, not stories of the tribal past. Their Hectors and Didos are all forgotten. The possibility that any nonhuman species possesses the capability for language is marginal at best. We alone are aware of our history and our ultimate destiny.

Yet even if this is so, one may still ask, must it be so? Could some other form be contrived that possessed such human characteristics? From ancient times, human beings have imagined machines—mechanical servants—that would do as bidden. For those who like to speculate about the future, such artifacts are fascinating. Perpetuum mobile machines are part of the wishful thinking of some. Robots to vacuum the carpet and wax the kitchen floor stir the hopes of others. Or if one wants to be expansive, one might wish for a robot to cook, clean, and even manage the household or a business; or perhaps a robot to talk to or confide in or one to give advice or act as a great source of knowledge, understanding, and wisdom.

Whether fact or fancy, exactly what class of object is it that is to be created? Would a robot that could carry on a conversation about Wittgenstein or angels be just a machine? Or do we also see ourselves as just machines? If, in the room the robots come and go, talking of Michelangelo, how should they be classified in relationship to man? Would such machines possess self-awareness? This feature of self-awareness or self-consciousness, which is at present restricted to man, seems to have at least a potential counterpart. However different in structure a human and a computer may be, perhaps the manner of discourse would be similar. Over the telephone, could one distinguish between a person and such a machine? Near the interface, the edges blur.

While the nature of *Homo sapiens* and computer may be so divergent as to elicit no true comparison, the potential for insight into either by studying the other is too great to ignore. It is revealing to compare how we have come to know something of the fundamental structure of each. While physicists and biologists appear to be at opposite ends of the natural science spectrum, each group has directed much effort toward understanding ultimate structures and origins. The successes of a combined reduction/synthesis approach to hierarchical problems are exemplified in such widely different areas as molecular biology and modern electronics. As the beginning point of their study of life, biologists had to take readily accessible, highly complex, fully functional forms of life. Joining forces with physicists and chemists in their search for the sources of form and function, they were ultimately led to a profound design at the microscopic level.

Physicists, on the other hand, beginning with bits of inert matter, had to learn to control these materials and impose their own design. Surpassing the alchemists' dream of transmuting the elements (which had been achieved years earlier by nuclear physicists), physicists breathed into that silicon clay something akin to life. Scientists immediately began to nurture and impress more complex designs on this new form. It developed in a niche where there was little competition and has evolved with a rapidity unequaled in the history of technology.

Modern computers were formed by human hands starting with a microscopic interface, an electronically controllable junction, an edge between dissimilar materials. (Despite its initial successes, an earlier vacuum tube line was unable to compete when solid state devices came to occupy the same niche, and the vacuum tube line became extinct.) These two complex information-transforming systems are radically different.

Living creatures emerged from the primordial ooze—organic objects able to reproduce. They exist suspended in a delicate balance between an internal coding system that results in the generation of a population whose members have slightly different characteristics and an environment to which living creatures must learn to correspond. Computers, on the other hand, are mechanical manufactured objects. They have no analog to organic growth: constructing a machine is not parallel to growth nor is the addition of memory or other peripherals. Computer structures are imposed from without, while organic structures take their form from within.

Few discoveries have had such impact on our understanding of life and our own nature as the deliniation of the structure of DNA. If there were an advance in our understanding of the brain, comparable to that of comprehending the structure of DNA, this new revelation would have as profound an influence on our understanding of our human nature as did Watson and Crick's discovery.

Few inventions have had such an impact on technology as the transistor. In a study of the hierarchy of understanding related to digital electronics, one must span the range from the fundamental theoretical substructure, the theory of quantum mechanics, to solid state physics and on to matters of logic and architecture. Possibly, continuing research on the most complex aspects of these electronic structures and successful development of the allied fields of artificial intelligence (AI) and cognitive psychology may provide another avenue for questions about the nature of understanding and our own nature.

Standing on the deck of an ocean liner on the open sea, one can see something of where one has been and, barring disaster, where one will be during the next hour or two. The limitations are in part a matter of curvature. At any point in history, one finds oneself on a curve with the forward view shrouded in the mists of as yet unformed space-time while the geologic wake churns up only a limited set of "fossils" to give evidence of the past. From the vantage point of the present, a look into the recent technological past reveals that modern electronics has become a dominant "family," the computer, the leading genus, with new and more powerful "species" evolving with great rapidity.

How are we affected by this new development? Our intelligence and flexibility have given us a clear status in the world of the living. But our view of our place in the universe has changed with time. We were once thought to be at the center of the universe, but Copernicus set forth an idea that was destablilizing, and Kepler's laws demolished the crystalline spheres. The destruction was devastating for those whose world view was formed around this concept. Man was cast adrift, sent off to the undistinguished sidelines, but still chosen. Human beings were once thought to have been specially created, formed from clay and rib, but Darwin and Wallace, together with Mendel, made such an approach untenable. The thought that through descent we are connected to echinoderms and even lower forms of life sets us still further adrift. Yet there are consolations; we find uniqueness in our intelligence and self-awareness, in our ability to use language and symbols. Can a mere tool, albeit a symbol-manipulating tool, cause still further estrangement? At the heart of the computer, there is no key idea comparable to gravity or natural selection. There is no central thought that provides a fulcrum about which one can shift a world view. What leverage the computer does have to challenge man's present unique position remains to be seen.

D. D.

1. *Why People Think Computers Can't*

MARVIN MINSKY

To guess the future, one must be a magician. The usual way is to walk backward into the past and then run forward again, hoping that a running start somehow makes a straight line. No reason it should. When I tried to think about the future of AI by examining the past, I found that AI was just like anything else: if you have some idea of what you want to find, you probably can find it by choosing the right place in the past, which makes this way of predicting history too easy to work very well. But let's try it anyway.

The people who built the first computers were scientists and engineers concerned with large numerical computations. Computers were so named because they could do arithmethic much faster than people; someday that will be seen as a funny historical accident. The first really useful computers appeared in the early 1950s. Even before that, a small group of people were thinking about what is now called information processing or symbol manipulation. These people realized that machines would be able to manipulate not only numbers but *symbols* as well: computers would be useful not only for arithemetic, but also to simulate theories about information and control processes in animals. At first, this was called cybernetics, a word that died out in the United States around 1960 but is still popular in other countries. The earliest computer programs included several experiments that would now be called AI. In the early 1950s, Alan Turing began a chess program, Anthony Oettinger wrote a learning program, and Russell Kirsch wrote a vision program—all using the machines that were designed just for arithmetic.

In the early days most people thought AI was impossible. Today, with the Star Wars robots *R2-D2* and *C*-Threepio, most people consider AI more advanced than it is. Even many computer scientists were dubious about artificial intelligence. Perhaps because they were so close to these machines, computer scientists felt they could clearly see that nothing could be inside computers except little electric currents: how could computers contain anything like a mind or a self? Many scientists argued that no machine could ever be *creative* or that computers do only what they are programmed to do. Familiarity bred contempt.

Today it is clear that computers *can* do much more than their programmers tell them to—in every practical sense. The first computer programs were simple lists of commands: Do this. Do that. Do this again. But soon, new kinds of programming were developed. Newell, Shaw, and Simon developed programs of bodies of advice such as, "If the difference between what you have and what you want is of kind *D*, then try to change it by using method *M*." Victor Yngve at M.I.T. developed programs that were bodies of statements such as, "If the situation turns out to be of such-and-such a form, then change it in such-and-such a way." Today, we are beginning to make systems that learn, that see which former experience in memory is most analogous to the present problem, and then use methods like those that worked best on similar problems in the past. When one uses these methods, it makes little sense to say that computers do only what they are told to do. Programmers may have no clear idea of what will happen, because they cannot anticipate all the interacting consequences of such fragments of knowledge and advice. They may not know much about the situations the machine will encounter in the future—or what things it might remember from its past.

Using such techniques, we have learned ways of programming computers to solve problems by trial and error. Now we are on the threshold of more ambitious experiments where programs will write new programs for themselves, with the goal of becoming even better at problem solving and learning. Clearly, there was something wrong with the old idea that machines could never, by their nature, create anything very new. But instead of boring the reader with technical speculations about the next generation of more intelligent machines, most of this chapter will try instead only to understand why so many people made so many wrong guesses about such things.

COULD COMPUTERS BE CREATIVE?

We naturally admire our Einsteins and Beethovens and want to know whether any computer could create such phenomenally original theories or such wondrous symphonies and quartets. But most people are sure that such creativity requires some mysterious gift that simply cannot be explained. (Then, the argument might go, no computer could do it, since, presumably, anything computers do can be explained.)

It is a mistake, though, to focus on only those things our culture regards as truly outstanding. For unless we first understand how people do ordinary things, we will fall into a trap: if we don't understand how ordinary people write ordinary symphonies, how can we possibly expect to understand how great composers write great symphonies—or even guess whether there is any special difficulty in creating symphonies? Of course, they seem mysterious, so first we have to understand the ordinary, both in terms of people and computers, to see how either one may ever come to have what we call ordinary common sense. Then, and only then, can we ask intelligent questions about the nature of the things we think require genius.

Why, in the first place, would we suppose that outstanding minds are any different, except in matters of degree, from ordinary minds? Of course, a genius must be intensely concerned with his or her domain (but this can be unconscious). He must become very proficient in it (but not necessarily in any articulate, academic sense); he must be tenaciously resistant to peer pressure, and so on. But none of these necessities demands a fundamental, qualitative difference. We may have another kind of reason for believing there are heroes with magical powers, but we should not let romantic hero worship confuse the nature of creativity with the social value of its products. As I see it, any ordinary person who can understand an ordinary conversation must have, already, in his head most of what our greatest thinkers have. Ordinary common sense already includes most of the skills that, better balanced, can make a genius.

If we look at only the surface of the skills that creative people use, we see only, perhaps, a greater diversity of skills and surer mastery. But underneath, there also has to lie administrative skills to knit those basic skills together. Is there a real difference? A good composer has to master many skills of phrase and theme—but those abilities are shared, to some degree, by everyone who speaks coherently. A good composer masters greater variations of form, but those skills, too, are shared by everyone who knows how to tell a story well. What only seems unusual is the total mass of different kinds of expertise, including skills of knowing how to use the other skills. For many people learn many skills, but only a few command enough of them to reach the vanguard. Some artists master fine detail but not the larger forms that make their pieces hang together, while other artists master larger forms but not the small ones. And then culture sets its threshold of acclamation, so that (no matter how great or small the differences among contestants) only a few individuals rise above the rest and are declared to possess that mysterious first-rank creativity. It may be fitting to make heroes of those who cross those somewhat arbitrarily defined thresholds, but until proven otherwise, we should not burden our philosophy with talk of inexplicability. There must be better ways of dealing with feelings of regret at having been labeled second-rate.

Still, there may indeed be a secret to what first-raters do, and I think the secret lies not in the surface skills themselves, but in the way that certain people *learn* so many more skills and a greater depth of skill! (See question 11 and responses.) The special, distinctive thing about "creative masters" is the way in which they choose *what* to learn: *they learn about learning*. Creativity begins with just one simple difference: our heroes of accomplishment are those who happen (at some early age) to aim an ordinary learning skill not at the usual surface tasks, but *at learning itself*. Once focused on learning, some become better and better at it. Then having found better ways of learning, these people find it easier than others to acquire more sets of skills, and these differences are magnified until there seems to be an awesome, qualitative difference. According to this view, first-rank creativity is just the consequence of childhood accidents where a person's ability to learn becomes a little more "self-applied" than usual.

Why do so many intelligent people, especially philosophers and humanists, go to great lengths to find something that human beings can do that machines cannot—to find some quality in themselves that cannot be duplicated in machines? Some even ask if a computer can make mistakes, as though they hoped that, somehow, the ability to err itself might be some precious gift. I have often heard, "I can see how a machine can solve a problem that you give it, but can a machine invent its *own* problems? Isn't the hard problem, really, to figure out what problem to solve?" But it is usually much easier to think of problems than to solve them. Of course, *sometimes* it is hard to find exactly the right question to ask, but even that is just another difficult problem, not necessarily an especially difficult *kind* of problem.

It is a waste of energy, today, to search for ways in which men differ from machines, because we simply know too little about how human minds really work. So instead of searching for things that machines cannot possibly do, I ask instead: *why are people so very inept at making theories about what they themselves can (or cannot) do*? In fact, although people think machines may be incapable of originality, there is actually no technical problem at all involved in making machines do things that no one ever told them to. In principle, we can program even the simplest computer to produce an infinite variety of different programs and then run them. Of course, most of them would be silly, and *that* is the real problem, the basic problem of all art and science: not to find variety and diversity, but to control and constrain them. Anyone, or any machine, can find the most bizarre, unthinkable extremes of novelty—

which is why the most valued kinds of originality are those that find small, subtle, useful variants of ordinary things.

Our most serious problems in machine intelligence today are *not* those of traditional humanist concern, such as creativity, intuition, and originality. What we need most to understand now is ordinary common sense! Many people seem to think this is an easy problem, already understood, just a matter of logic, and so forth. It isn't. Many people seem to think that understanding the intellect must be easy compared to establishing theories on such arcane matters as emotion. These people have things turned around: we know a great deal about emotion but little about thinking, which is really the more complicated of the two. Perhaps emotion *seems* more important, but we must realize that this may be a trick, in which an emotion is only doing its job!

MUST COMPUTERS BE LOGICAL?

In 1956, Newell, Shaw, and Simon wrote a computer program that was quite good at finding proofs of theorems in mathematical logic. In fact, their program proved all the theorems in the first volume of Russell and Whitehead's *Principia Mathematica*, including some that are quite difficult even for today's college students. The program actually found some rather novel proofs. So in a sense, we know how to make machines do logical reasoning, but I don't see this as a big step toward understanding how people do common-sense reasoning.

Our culture is addicted to theories that divide minds into two parts. In one such theory, the first half of the mind is logical, rational, and sort of brittle, while the second half is soft, vague, and sort of intuitive. (See question 6 and responses.) Variations of this theory are so ill-defined that they are almost impossible to tell apart: logic vs. intuition, spatial vs. verbal, quantitative vs. qualitative, local vs. global, reason vs. emotion. Now, there is nothing wrong in starting with two-part theories if we use them as steps toward better theories. But if we end up that way, we usually have just one idea instead of two—whatever it is—vs. everything else. Our culture's mental-pair distinctions are limited in this way, and I doubt they have much value as theories of the mind. Perhaps they are only symptoms of some inability to cope with more than one idea at a time.

In any case, these age-old distinctions between logic and intuition, or reason and emotion, have been the basis of many unsound arguments about machine intelligence. It was clear from AI's earliest days that logical deduction would be easy to program. Accordingly, people who believed that thinking was mainly logical were led to expect that computers would soon do the sorts of things they believed people used logic for. Most people also assumed that it would be much more difficult, and perhaps impossible, to program more qualitative traits, such as intuition, metaphor, esthetics, or reasoning by analogy. I wasn't among them.

In 1964, a student of mine, T. G. Evans, wrote a program that showed how computers could actually use analogies to do some interesting kinds of reasoning about perception of geometric structures. This program made some humanistic skeptics so angry that they wrote papers about it. One paper threw out the baby with the bath by arguing that if a machine could do analogical reasoning, well, then, that kind of reasoning must not be so important. Another complained that Evans's program was too complicated to be the basis of an interesting psychological theory, because it used about 60,000 computer instruction words (which suggests that there wasn't a baby in the first place).

Nevertheless, Evans's program showed how wrong it was to assume that computers could do only logical or quantitative reasoning. Why had so many people made this same mistake? I see it as a curious irony: all those people had mistaken *their own personal limitations* for limitations of computers! That is, because most people hadn't been able to establish sensible theories of how they themselves could reason by analogy, they were led to suppose that no well-defined mechanism could exist that did so, hence, no computer or program could do it! That is why it was left to AI researchers (instead of psychologists or philosophers) to establish the first plausible theories of reasoning by analogy and hence be able to make computers do such things!

COULD COMPUTERS EVER REALLY UNDERSTAND THINGS?

"I see you have programmed that computer to obey verbal commands. You have probably inserted into its memory what it should do in response to each command. *But I don't believe the program really understands the words in any human sense*." (See question 1 and responses.) This popular criticism was quite valid when applied to the well-known "psychiatrist program" Eliza; it doesn't apply to, say, Daniel Bobrow's program for solving high school algebra word problems. That program understood just enough English to work the kinds of word problems that most students find very hard. It is not very difficult to learn to solve the kinds of equations we encounter in high school algebra. But word problems are difficult because the program (or the student) has to figure out what equations to write down. Bobrow's program wasn't half bad at that.

Did Bobrow's program really understand the words? Is *understand* even an idea we can ask science to deal with? We don't have to define words like *mean* and *understand*, just because philosophers have tried to do that for thousands of years! Such words are only *social objects*; if they lead to good ideas, fine, but in this case, I doubt that they point out significant distinctions, and I suspect that they only handicapped our predecessors who tried very hard to figure out what meanings were or how they are connected to words. But that is a misguided ambition anyway, similar to expecting people to agree on what *good* means, without considering the individual psychology of each person who uses the word.

To see how desperate philosophers have become, consider today's most popular philosophical theory of meaning—an idea called model theory. What does it mean to say that Boston is in Massachusetts? According to model theory, this means the set of all possible worlds in which (1) there is a Boston and a Massachusetts and (2) that Boston is actually in that Massachusetts! This begs the question of what meaning means, because it gives no hint of how to recognize whether something in a "possible world" is actually a "Boston" or not. Yet it is taken quite seriously, because no other theory has accumulated so respectable a mathematical tradition.

WHAT IS A NUMBER?

We cannot discuss meaning without discussing the meaning of something, so let us discuss the meaning of some particular number, say, five. No one would claim that Bobrow's algebra program could be said to understand what numbers really are, nor would one say that about Slagle's calculus program, which I will discuss later. Yet both programs "know" arithmetic in the sense of finding correct sums like five plus seven is twelve. The trouble is that neither program understands—in any *other* sense—what either five or seven or twelve are, or, for that matter, what *plus* or *is* is. Well, suppose I asked the reader what five is? I will bet that the secret lies in that little word *other*!

Early in this century, Russell and Whitehead proposed to tell us how to define a number (in that same book, *Principia Mathematica*). *Five*, according to them, is *the set of all possible sets that each have five members*. That includes this set of five ballpoint pens and that litter of five kittens. I suppose it also includes this set of five words and even the five things most difficult of all to think of. Unfortunately, funny examples like those caused inconsistencies and paradoxes, so the theory had to be doctored to avoid them; in its final form, it became too complicated for practical use.

In my view, there is no need to try to capture meanings in such a standard, public sort of way. In fact, as I will show, that defeats our real purposes, because it is a mistake to ignore a fundamental psychological fact: what something means to me depends to some extent on everything else I know, and no one else knows just those things in just those ways. I maintain that a psychologically useful theory of meanings, even of something as widely understood as *five*, needs some built in way of dealing with differences between different knowers. Most of my friends who are scientists hate this idea, because they fear that if each meaning depends on the mind it is in, and on all the other meanings in that mind, then there isn't any place to start. They fear that if meanings are that private, then there is no way of breaking into the closed circle of the mind, and everything becomes too subjective to be scientific.

However, there *is*, indeed, a scientific way of handling this: We can start a new set of theories about the circles themselves! We don't *have to* break into them—*we only have to have sound theories about them*. Former theories try to suppress the ways that meanings depend on one another (and how one mind can differ from another). The trouble is that this approach loses all the power and richness of those circles! In fact, we actually don't *want* to get ourselves inside those circles. It is a futile dream to hope to be absolutely sure of understanding something exactly the way someone else does. The ideal of perfect, foolproof communication was just a fantasy to begin with; the only way to understand precisely what someone else thinks we mean at every level of nuance is to become just like that person. But that isn't what we want either, because then in that new state of existence we couldn't know what it was that we in our original state had been trying to communicate, and so on.

COULD A COMPUTER UNDERSTAND WHAT A NUMBER IS?

What would it mean to say that *five* does not mean a simple, isolated thing, but a web or network of interdependent processes? Well, let us proceed with that example. One way to know when we have five things is to recite one, two, three, four, five, while pointing to the different things. Of course, while doing this, we have to (1) touch each thing once and (2) not touch any twice. An easy way to do *that* is to pick up one object as we repeat each counting-word, and remove it. Children learn to do is in their minds or, when there are too many objects to keep track of, to use some physical device, such as pointing.

There are many, many other ways of understanding *five*. We could keep a standard set of five things somewhere, then match some *other* set of things to them one to one: If everything matches, and nothing is left over, then we would have five. We could use our fingers as that standard set of things.

Another way of understanding *five* is to arrange objects into groups of two and three. Again, we can group them mentally, without actually moving them. Or we can lay out the objects on a table to form a square with one in the middle; that makes five, too. Note that we might acquire this meaning of *five* before understanding *two* or *three*. I knew a child who was quite proficient with hexagons long before she knew much about *four* or *five*.

Which of these methods—counting, matching, grouping, and so forth—provides the real meaning of *five*? How silly; each supports the others to make a useful, versatile system of skills. Neither chicken nor egg need come first; they both evolve from something else.

Mathematicians and philosophers despise such interconnected networks; they prefer simple "chains" of definitions where each new thing depends only on other things that have been previously defined. In my theory, the ordinary, common-sense meaning of *five* is no single link in any chain of definitions. Instead, the word *five* activates the entire network of different ways of recognizing five things, using them, remembering them, comparing them, and so forth. Such networks are useful for solving problems, because there are so many different ways that we won't become stuck when one of them doesn't work. If we can't make one of our ideas about five do the job, in a certain context, we can switch to one of the others. If we followed the mathematicians' approach, we would be completely stuck if we got into the slightest trouble.

By the way, why *do* mathematicians prefer chains to nets? Why would they want each thing to depend on as few other things as possible—instead of as many as possible? The answer is a nice paradox. Things are done that way in mathematics in order to assure that if anything at all is incorrect, then everything else will collapse! To a mathematician, that sort of fragility is *good*, not bad, because it helps detect if *any single thing* that is believed is inconsistent with any others. This kind of reasoning ensures absolute consistency, which is fine for mathematics, but terrible for real life, where there are *always* things that we believe which aren't really true.

Perhaps this helps explain how we manage to make almost all our children afraid of mathematics! We imagine that it makes it easy for them to see what is right by arranging for everything to go utterly wrong almost all the time!

To learn about numbers (or anything else), children must build networks, not towers. Two hands and two feet and two shoes: We learn those first in terms of symmetry and matching, not counting. We soon learn also that when we count two or three things, we get the same number each time. We also know about threes from rhymes and stories about three pigs or bears or turtle doves (whatever they might be). And notice how many different kinds of three are found in those innocent fairy tales! The three bears themselves are two and one: mother and father and child. But those bears' three bowls of food make quite a different kind of three:—too hot vs. too cold vs. just right; this three is a *compromise between two extremes*. So, too, were these bears' forbidden beds: too hard, too soft, and just right. The child in the real world learns many different threes, related to each other in many different, interesting ways. It is a large network. The meaning is the entire network, not a mere node, and there is no basic three that the others depend on.

Is there a paradox in this? If each meaning depends on several other meanings, then don't we have a castle built on air? Well, yes and no. There is nothing really wrong with circular definitions where each part gives the others more meaning: what is wrong with liking two tunes, for example—each one the more because it contrasts with the other? The entire mind is, in this sense, a castle in the air; what is wrong with that? One objection then would be that there is no connection with reality. But that isn't really a practical problem, because our sensory and motor brain machinery ensure at least some infantile relationship between our perceived objects and some physical reality. Still, this is only a matter of degree, and to a really large extent, minds *can* become detached and build (and share) imaginary worlds for better or for worse.

Let us return to earth. I will agree that no computer could understand what a number is if it were forced to have only one way to deal with numbers, such as adding them up. But neither could any child, psychologist, or philosopher understand numbers under that constraint. Thus, it isn't a matter of computers at all. Our culture has become caught up in the search for meanings that can stand by themselves, outside of *any* mental context, and there is no reason to suppose that such abstractions can exist. Thus, we are not dealing with any special limitation of computers. The reason so many people feel computers cannot understand is that their own conception of understanding is so shallow and simplistic that, of course, no machine could understand in *that* way—nor could a person, either! We cannot have real meaning until we join together many partial meaning structures. If we have only one of them, then we don't have any meaning. That is why those seeking true meanings never find them!

COULD A COMPUTER BE AWARE OF ITSELF?

> Even if a computer does something, it is just mechanical. The computer cannot feel; it can't be conscious. It simply has no self to feel things with. How could a computer ever really know what we mean when we tell it that "Boston is in Massachusetts"?

I wonder what *you* suppose happens in your head when I say something like that to you. Do you understand it? I will demonstrate that here, again, the problem doesn't actually concern computers at all; it doesn't even concern understanding. The problem concerns *you*. It isn't that you doubt that computers can think; the problem is that you don't really believe that thinking is possible at all! In fact, the problem is that little word *you* itself.

We have a verb *understand*, so we feel there must be some agent to do the understanding, someone inside our head to do the understanding. Now it is perfectly all right when we speak to each other for me to call that someone you and for you to call it me. That's fine for social purposes. But everything goes awry when we try to apply that social idea in a technical-scientific context, because it makes us forget there must be some substantial structure inside that you or me *to do the work*. That social idea makes us assume that there is some single, simple, self inside our head instead of those enormous, intricate webs of which we spoke earlier.

How does this idea of self lead people to believe that machines can never think? I believe it happens this way. When I tell something to a computer, it computes something. In order to understand what I tell it, the computer must compute a meaning. Then in order to understand the meaning, the computer must transmit it to something like a self. But since I am dealing with a computer, it cannot have a self anything like mine; it can only compute. So, at best, a computer can only simulate a self. To do that, it must compute something, and so forth. In other words, for a machine to think, it would need a self, which would need another self, and so on. The infinite series of selves each pass the job of real understanding to the next.

What is wrong? The same thing again: this imaginary limitation of computers has nothing to do with computers at all but comes from not having an idea of how *people* really work or feel, or think. To put it firmly, that skepticism about computer intelligence emerges from our unconscious suspicion that *thinking* (intelligent or otherwise) is itself impossible!

Perhaps that suspicion is almost justified: it certainly would seem that people are *not* very proficient at thinking—or at least at thinking about thinking. And there is an irony in this. Why, indeed, were our old theories about thinking so inadequate? It was precisely *because* we hadn't started to understand well enough what computers—that is, what complicated mechanisms—*can* do! For (in my view, anyway) there seems no attractive alternative to believing that brains are made of very technically complicated machinery. Therefore, we need advanced computational theories before we can expect to understand how the brain works. Naturally, the old theories from precomputer eras of mechanism science made little progress. It was presumptuous to suppose we could understand anything as complicated as thinking without doing any hard, technical work.

We now need better theories about how to understand the complex webs of processes that work within the huge networks that we build to interconnect all our fragments of knowledge. To understand, say, the concept of number, a child must connect a myriad of different ways of counting and measuring and comparing. Within those webs, some processes or programs have to run, and we must never count on any single process to suffice, since nothing ever works out exactly as we hope. Such theories are today just a gleam in the eye. Still, several projects are now starting to work on ways of weaving such complex multiprocess webs.

COULD A COMPUTER HAVE COMMON SENSE?

Back to predicting the future by examining the past. In retrospect, I see how this field seems to have evolved in a funny backward direction. Is it not odd that the very earliest AI programs excelled at advanced, adult subjects. I have already mentioned the program written in 1956 that was quite good at certain kinds of mathematical logic. In 1961, J. R. Slagle wrote a program that solved college calculus problems, using symbols rather than numbers—just the sort of problems, using symbols rather than numbers—just the sort of problems that M.I.T. freshmen were doing at that time. The program got an *A* on an exam. A few years later, D. Bobrow developed that first program that could solve high school algebra problems. In 1970, Terry Winograd wrote a computer program that didn't do grown-up mathematics at all; it only worked with children's building blocks. This program could stack up blocks, pull them down, rearrange them, and put them in boxes. And it had much more ability than previous programs to understand English.

It took us many years before we could make computers do some of the things that any six-year-old can do. Now we know from Piaget's studies of the growth of children's thinking that children usually learn the formal kinds of thinking required for calculus or algebra long after they master many other kinds of reasoning. Why were we able to make AI programs do such grown-up things so long before we could make them do childish things? Is it possible that adult thinking is somehow simpler than children's?

Winograd's program could even converse with the person operating it, in order to answer questions about what it was doing, and how, using something very much like standard English. Still, we should wonder why—if Slagle's program could solve college-level problems in 1961—it took a decade longer to write a program that was able only to play, like a child, with simple blocks and boxes? The answer is that it often requires more to be a novice than an expert, because, sometimes, the things an expert has to know can be quite few and simple—although it may be very difficult to discover (or learn) them in the first place. The entire knowledge network built into Slagle's program, which contains much of what the college student has to learn about integration, has only about one hundred facts, perhaps twenty rules about calculus, and fifty rules about algebra. Perhaps most important, the program has about a dozen ways of telling *which of two calculus problems is probably the easier.* This is important because these procedures embody the kind of knowledge we call judgment, without which we can only flounder. The driving force in Slagle's program was the process that decided what to try next. By 1961, we knew enough about that sort of thing for Slagle to build his calculus program, and today we know enough about such heuristics to build routinely many other useful kinds of expert problem-solving programs.

However, while we know how to write such programs for special applications, we don't yet know enough about such matters to build good common-sense problem-solving programs—for example, programs that can do most things young children do. Winograd's work showed some new ways of assembling many different kinds of knowledge about shapes and colors, syntax, space and time, and problem-solving processes. Only in that way were we able to make a program do what everyone thought was much easier than calculus—playing with children's blocks. To make things work inside his child's world of building blocks, Winograd needed about a thousand knowledge fragments in his network, whereas Slagle needed only a hundred. The problem, as I see it, is that experts can often manage with deep but narrow bodies of knowledge. However, common-sense thinking is technically more complicated, because although the reasoning may be much shallower, it needs many different kinds of knowledge, and each kind of knowledge may need different kinds of processes. And, then, the more different kinds of processes, the more types of interactions between them, and so on.

But Winograd's contribution was not merely a matter of quantity: he had to invent *different kinds* of heuristic knowledge and new ways for them to control and exploit each other. He used a new kind of programming, called heterarchy, as opposed to the hierarchy used in previous programs and theories. Although less centralized, there was more interaction and interruption between parts in this system: while one part was trying to parse a sentence, another part would be trying to make the grammar compatible with the meaning. As soon as one part of the program guessed that *pick* was a verb (as in *pick up the block*), another program part might check to see if block were really the sort of thing that could be picked up. I believe that what we call common sense requires a lot of just that kind of switching from one viewpoint to another, involving different kinds of ideas.

COULD A COMPUTER BE CONSCIOUS?

When people ask if a machine can be self-conscious, they always seem to expect the answer to be no. I propose to shock the reader by explaining why machines may be capable, in principle, of possessing even more and better consciousness than people have.

Let us begin by asking someone quite seriously whether any one can really be self-aware. He will surely answer that of course people can, because they are. Then I will say that I meant it literally: Can we be aware of everything that happens in our mind? He says yes or no, but most likely he will say that he didn't mean *that*—he meant something else. I continue: What do you mean by self-aware if not aware of what happens inside you? He will probably say that he didn't mean aware *of* what's *in* himself, just aware *of* himself. Then I will look puzzled, ask what that means, and if he is like everyone else I've met, he will say something like: It is really very hard to explain—and start to look for some way to get away (and so will I).

Why is it that our alleged self-awareness can say so very little about itself? I think the answer is that it is misnamed. Although the phenomenon that we call self-awareness is very useful and important, it really cannot do what people think it can. We all seem to assume that we have some faculty that enables us to discover (or perceive) true things about our minds. Instead, I think, we have only a certain limited ability, sometimes, to make useful *guesses* about reasons and explanations of why and how the mind works. And while these guesses, products of our vaunted self-awareness, are often very clever, they do not show any significant tendency to be profoundly correct! Our insight into how we think is no neat window on the truth: it doesn't even seem to do so well as other ways we have of figuring out what is going on.

Accordingly, we should be able to provide our machines with a greater ability to establish theories about themselves. First, we should provide them with better access to their own trees of goals and values. Then we could begin to give them ways of constructing simple explanations of how their procedures work toward those ends. In fact, Winograd's program has already demonstrated one rather accurate, though somewhat shallow, way of doing this. The difficult part of the problem wouldn't be providing access to internal information; the difficult problem would be just the same problem we have yet to solve more generally—building programs with enough common sense to make good use of such insight. That is to say, our present programs are still too narrow and specialized to deal with anything as complicated as a theory of thinking. But as we learn to build more intelligent machines, I don't see any reason to anticipate difficulty in giving them correspondingly more self-insight—that is, if we decide that this is a wise thing to do. Perhaps we will even have to do so!

Most skeptics will admit that computers will probably continue to become more intelligent yet doubt that computers will ever be self-conscious. I am suggesting that these skeptics may have things precisely backward! Maybe at some point we will *have* to make computers more self-conscious in order to make them more intelligent! I think our culture's nonmechanical heritage teaches us that self-awareness is a mysterious metaphysical appendage, that somehow makes us human yet *has no fundamental use or function*. I suspect our ability to make crude models of ourselves is no mysterious luxury, but a necessary and practical device, because no problem solver can be robust enough without some insight into its own goals and motives! For example, a problem solver could not safely undertake any complex, long-range task unless it could ensure its own future concern with it, and this requires predicting our own dispositions. Nor can we expect to learn how to solve difficult, new kinds of problems without at least some elementary, simplified idea of how we already manage to solve easier, old problems.

Now technically, there are certain absolute, theoretical limitations to self-insight; for example, no machine of any kind can predict ahead of time what it will do by taking into account *all* the details of what its internal agencies are doing now. But these limitations are not interesting. Presumably, there are also practical limitations; people, for example, can relate hardly anything about the mechanisms of their thinking. They are usually reduced to saying such things as, "I had an idea . . ." or "it occurred to me that. . . ." Of course, we often hear of mystical experiences where someone claims some sense of total, utterly complete understanding. However, such people can say so very little more of what they learned that we can conclude only that what they learned was how to extinguish the question-asking portion of their mind. All this leads me to suspect that what we call self-consciousness does not live up to its reputation of profound revelation. Instead, it seems to provide only a sketchy, simplified mind model, suitable for mundane, practical, and social uses. In fact, it would seem that correct technical details of our mental operations are so inaccessible to our selves as to be counterintuitive: such important discoveries as Freud's unconscious and Piaget's conservation met strong resistance until nonintrospective evidence overruled those incorrect intuitions. (See questions 2, 3, and responses.)

When and if we choose to build more artfully conceived intelligent machines, we should have many new options that were not available during the brain's evolution, for the biological constraints of vertebrate evolution must have dictated many details of the interconnections of our brains. In the new machines, we will be able to provide whatever paths we wish. Though the new machines still cannot possibly keep track in real time of everything they do, we surely should be able (at least in principle) to make those new, synthetic minds vastly more self-conscious than we are, in the sense of being more profound and having insightful knowledge about their own nature and function. Thus, in the end, those new creatures should have more interesting and richer inner lives than do people. Treason, you say. I suppose we will have to leave these decisions to future generations: they won't *have* to build things that well unless they want to.

COULD WE BUILD TRULY INTELLIGENT MACHINES?

There is absolutely no known technical reason to doubt that we could build truly intelligent machines. It may take a very long time, though, to learn enough about common-sense reasoning to make machines with manlike versatility. We already know some ways of making useful, specialized, expert systems. We don't yet know that many ways of making these systems learn enough to improve themselves in interesting ways. However, there are already some ideas about this topic on the scientific horizon.

On the other side, every one of the assertions about what machines can never do but people can are only foolish speculations. We simply do not yet know enough about how human minds work to make such arguments. The proponents of such theories are either simply bluffing or making obscure technical mistakes. Accordingly, I recommend that instead of being tricked into thinking that such arguments make sense, we simply regard them as opportunities to see more ways in which human minds can err! I am serious: the better we understand why minds do foolish things, the better prepared we will be to figure out how, also, they so often do things well.

In years to come, we will learn more ways of making machines behave sensibly. (See question 12 and responses.) We will learn more about new kinds of knowledge and processes and how to use them to make still more new knowledge. We will come to think of learning and thinking and understanding not as mysterious, single, special processes, but as entire worlds of ways to represent and transform ideas. In turn, those new ideas will suggest new machine architectures, and they in turn will further change our ideas about ideas. No one can now tell where all these new ideas will lead. One thing is certain, though: there must be something wrong with any reasoned claim today to know any fundamental differences between men and possible machines. And there is a simple reason why such arguments must be erroneous: we simply do not know enough yet about the real workings of either men or possible machines.

2. *The Problem of Natural Language*

ROGER C. SCHANK

A typical popular conception of the computer of tomorrow is a machine with a master who sits there and says to it: "Computer do this"—and the computer does it. Everyone's popular conception of a computer scientist is someone concerned with mathematics or wiring diagrams. Actually, these two things don't mix very well. In fact, what we would really like to create is a computer that is able to speak and listen. Curiously, achieving these goals is neither a problem of mathematics nor wiring. The question is: what is it a problem of?

Consider language. Given the state of the current environment, most contemporary thought about language is dominated by linguists (see questions 9, 10, and responses), which is obvious on the one hand but unfortunate on the other. The unfortunate part is that when we think about language, we tend to think about grammar, because that is what we were taught to think about. When we want to learn a language, we are taught grammar. When we reach the point of being able to put some rules on a machine, we consider what rules we have, and the answer is grammatical rules. A lot of time was wasted in computer science, and particularly in AI, thinking about how to put the grammars into these machines. Unfortunately, the question of grammar isn't the question that we want to consider.

What we want to do is make this machine understand. It is not exactly obvious what we should do to solve that problem. My approach has been to try to figure out how humans understand, on the ground that they are an existence proof. At the very least, we know people understand, so what we want to do is to figure out how they do it, then see if we can make computers do the same thing. (See questions 1–3 and responses.) Now this may sound as though we were going to run psychological experiments, but that wouldn't work either. The experiments are likely to provide a set of isolated facts within the confines of the experiment, and that is not what we want to consider.

We want a more general approach to the problem of how understanding works, and that is too vast to try to control in a psychological laboratory. In a sense, we are trying to solve a problem for which there is no paradigm but AI provides some direction. The procedure is to postulate some mechanisms, write a program that follows those rules, and then check to see if that program does what we want it to do. If the answer is almost always no, then the program must be modified. That loop, modifying the program after having built it after having devised the theory, followed by creating a new theory as a result of a failed program, is pretty much what AI consists of.

The fundamental problem is meaning. If we want to obtain meaning from a text, there are several problems that must be dealt with. In fact, there are several distinct classes of these problems; they include synonomy, paraphrase, translation, inference, and ambiguity. Let us consider the problem of paraphrase. We want to consider how we are able to paraphrase sentences when the exact words have been hopelessly forgotten. With regard to the computer, we don't want to store words in the computer; we want to store those things that will permit the machine to make paraphrases; the paraphrase problem is a key problem.

Another crucial area is the inference problem, which is related to the fact that we never say what we mean. We say bits of things that lead to what we mean. When I say that I am hungry, a perfectly good response is: that is an interesting condition of your body. However, people are expected to make inferences. It is maddening if they don't make inferences. One wants to say unpleasant things. I would expect the person to whom I have said, "I'm hungry"—if the person happens to be someone who is responsible for making dinner—to say that it will be ready in ten minutes or something along those lines. If it is someone who is delaying me on my way to a restaurant, and the conversation has led to something novel he'd say, "let's go to lunch." There are many ways of dealing with such problems, and they require making inferences.

What is an inference? It isn't what has been said, but what has to be figured out. Now, people become very annoyed when these inferences are not made. If people are going to talk to machines they'll become angry with them if machines cannot make the correct inferences.

Right from the beginning, we are involved not with a problem of grammar, but with a problem of figuring out other things. If we have to make inferences and if we have to make them based on just the meanings of the words, that poses a problem. Consider the word *give*; what does it mean? *John gave a party*; does that have any relationship to *John gave Mary a book* or *John gave Mary a hard time* or *John gave Mary a kiss* or *John gave up* or *John gave no reason for his actions*? What is the meaning of *give*? If we consider enough examples of how the word is used, we conclude that *give* doesn't have a meaning at all. This is a bit extreme; one sense of give, a sense which essentially everyone is willing to agree on, is a sort of transfer of possession of something. Another could be some sort of contract action.

Having studied these examples at some length, I have tried to construct a canonical form for meaning. A canonical form implies that no matter what the arrangement or organization is and no matter how stated, the meaning remains the same. Thus, I can use fifteen different paraphrases of the sentence *John punched Mary*, and they should all have the same content. First, let us consider the word *punch*, which has something to do with the physical contact between one person's fist and another person. Given this approach, we have identified a series of primitive actions of which PROPEL is one. PROPEL carries with it a set of cases that provides a frame from which to speak. It says that PROPEL implies that there is an actor, an action, and an object, which can be placed in a framework.

action:	PROPEL
actor:	John
object:	Fist
from:	John
to:	Mary

It is not unreasonable to ask if this method works. How many primitives like PROPEL are needed? The answer is only 11. Eleven primitive actions can express *all* human activities that there are in the world.

Primitive Actions

Mental Actions	Physical Actions	Instrumental Actions
MTRANS: transferring information from one person to another or from one part of the mind to another (John told Mary about the movie.)	PTRANS: transferring location (Mary went to the movie.)	ATTEND: directing a sense organ at some concrete object (Mary looked at the screen.)
MBUILD: transferring information into a person's conscious processor (Mary decided to	INGEST: taking an object to the inside of an organism (Mary ate some popcorn.)	SPEAK: producing sounds (Mary spoke.)
	PROPEL: applying a force (Mary threw some popcorn.)	MOVE: moving part of the body (Mary raised her hand.)
		GRASP: grasping an

see the movie.)
ATRANS: transferring possession
(Mary bought a ticket.)

object
(Mary held some popcorn.)
EXPEL: taking an object from inside an organism to the outside
(Mary cried at the end.)

These eleven actions cannot express nuances, which must be expressed by those things that indicate what else is true about actions. If we consider the expression *taking a bus*, it is not a transfer possession operation, but it can be mapped into the right format. Someone physically moves onto the bus, and the bus then transfers itself. Combinations of these operations will, in fact, express language.

One of the most important questions associated with representations of meaning is: Does this procedure depend on a specific language or is it language free? If it is language free, then that is very important. If the form into which the message has been set isn't English anymore, then I can build a program that will translate not only English into this representation, but also French, Spanish, Chinese, or whatever, and I can also get back into these languages.

The procedure in attacking a complicated problem is to break it up into manageable pieces. Ultimately though, we must have integration: We must be able to reassemble things in such a way as to regain meaning. Integration is very difficult unless we consider the whole as being constructed from pieces. Integration requires a control structure that says first do this and then do that and then that; we can do this with language, too. Language can be considered from a certain simplistic view as having three phases. The first phase is understanding: We take in an English sentence and obtain a meaning representation from it. The second phase is inference, when we try to figure out what else is true on the basis of that meaning. Meaning must be used as a basis, not words. The rules used to derive what is true when we punch somebody will be the same rules used to derive what is true when we hit somebody with our fist. Lastly, we want to generate; that is, we want to take these meanings and put the original or related ideas back into English.

Margie is a program that we built in the early 70s; what follows is an example of how it works. First, there is the problem of analysis. Given the sentence *John gave Mary a book*, what do we know about John? Initially, we must establish a frame. There is an actor, an action, an object, a to, and a from; we fill them in to be able to see interrelationships. What can be said about John? He may turn out to be the object in a passive sentence, but we guess that he is the actor. It is necessary to have the computer guess, which is neither mathematical nor formal, but people do it, so machines have to if they wish to understand. We guess that *gave* is ATRANS. Now if *gave* is ATRANS, we then expect *John* to fill the ACTOR slot. When Mary comes along, we will know something about her. The implication is that there is transfer of possession to another human being, and if Mary is a human being, she is going to fit into the TO slot, particularly if the word *to* is there. So we place Mary in that slot, and find we have an empty slot, the OBJECT. We can insert *book*, and the final representation becomes

actor:	John
action:	ATRANS
object:	book
to:	Mary
from:	John

John ATRANS object book to Mary from John.

Now the program just described would work for *Mary received a book from John*. Mary would initially be placed in the ACTOR slot but then moved to the OBJECT slot when we come to the word *received*, which is, not normally the form of an ATRANS. The same procedure would work on sentences like, *Mary took a book from John*, with only a slightly different representation (the ACTOR would be Mary), because the two sentences are not identical.

When two sentences are rather similar, it is important that they be analyzed in a manner which preserves similarity, because any rules derived from ATRANS will yield the same result for both sentences. (This is the very procedure that enables a computer program to make inferences.) Whether we say take, give, steal, or buy, some of the inferences will be the same. For example, the person who has taken the thing, stolen the thing, or bought the thing, now has it. The rule varies according to the words we are using, because it is a rule derived from a concept, that is, an ATRANS. The program Margie actually did the three things just mentioned: First, it placed the sentences into a case frame, then it made some inferences, and lastly it carried out some generation.

Clearly, these systems can become enormous structures. The previous example is only a "baby" structure; sentences can be much more involved. For example, if we had the sentence *John paid two dollars to the bartender for some wine*, Margie's analysis would indicate a reciprocal causality. The word *pay* is actually two ATRANSes, an ATRANS of *dollars* and an ATRANS of *wine.* If that structure is presented to the computer, it can produce 150 sentences that say the same thing; six of them are given:

John paid the bartender two dollars for some wine.

The bartender sold John some wine for two dollars.

John bought some wine from the bartender for two dollars.

John paid the bartender two dollars to give him some wine.

The bartender traded John some wine for two dollars.

The bartender gave John some wine, and he gave him two dollars.

How are these sentences generated? There are rules for inferring these structures. Two classes of rules are actually needed for reading structures. The first class reads them into language and the second reads them into memory in order to have them available for manipulation by other routines.

In inference mode, the program Margie is able to determine with high reliability things that are unsaid. For example, the sentence *John told Mary that Bill wants a book*, generates a set of inferences that the generator can use and then turn the code back into English again. So we would have:

John believes that Bill wants a book.

Mary now knows that Bill wants a book.

Bill wants a book.

Bill wants to come to possess the book.

Bill will probably want to read the book.

Bill might want to know the contents contained in the book.

What the machine is actually doing is thinking about the sentence. Now, I use the word *think* somewhat loosely and at the same time not all that loosely. We cannot understand if we don't start thinking, and those two acts are related. Understanding is not a passive formal process.

Let us consider a few more examples.

Bill might get himself a book.

John may want Mary to give Bill a book.

John and Mary may have been together recently.

This can continue in all sorts of ways. "John gave Mary a book. Oh, she's seeing him again." We can do that. The point, of course, is that the inference process is almost unconstrainable. We can go in any direction from any sentence.

The problem with our computer programs is that the inference process is similarly unconstrained: It goes in no particular direction and would cheerfully continue indefinitely. In fact, programming the machine to make inferences is not difficult; stopping it is tricky. The machine will go on endlessly, and the question is, "Now what do we do?"

I haven't defined inference very well, and I am not going to, but I will present an algorithm that can be used to figure out what an inference is. It is called the but test. The but test states that if the phrases *X* and *Y* are combined to form the sentence *X but Y* and it makes sense, we have an inference; *Y* is an inference from *X*. Therefore, if I say that John punched Mary, but his hand didn't touch her, the statement doesn't make sense. Is the concept "his hand touched her" an inference from the act of punching? No; it is part of the content, part of what punch means. Therefore, it has to be representated initially and not as part of the inference process.

If I say that John punched Mary, but it didn't rain, that doesn't make sense either but for entirely different reasons: The two sentences are simply not related. Consequently, it cannot be a legitimate inference because legitimate inferences make sense. *John punched Mary, but she didn't cry* and *John punched Mary, but they are still together* are legitimate inferences because they make sense even though we would normally assume that after having punched Mary, Mary would no longer be with John or that she would cry.

The but test is simply an heuristic; it provides some sense of what an inference is. An inference is what we tend to think would work, which leads us to wonder about the meaning of the word *but*. In English, *but* means negate the inference that first seemed appropriate, which is precisely how a computer "understands" that word.

I actually presented this concept to linguists ten to fifteen years ago. I used to ask them about the representation of the sentence *Mary gave John a book*, and they would say, "Mary gave book John." I would add that he is going to read it, which is not indicated explicitly but seemed to be implied by the sentence. Suppose I say that John likes books, what is the interpretation? That John likes books or he likes to what? It could mean that he likes to stack books. The trouble with inferences is that they can always be wrong, but that doesn't stop us from making them. Any sensible computer will not proceed by estimating probabilities. For example, the idea of proceeding by reasoning that there is a 25-percent chance John is going to read the book, a 32-percent chance he is going to hold the book and not read it, and so forth, simply doesn't work. A procedure like that cannot, in fact, communicate very well. Humans have a marvelous way of not caring about any of that. They just leap to conclusions. That is what we have our computer do, too.

As I pointed out earlier, the inference process is unconstrained. The question is, if it's unconstrained, what do we do? One possibility is to attempt to determine how people constrain. One way of constraining inferences involves using an item that we call a script. A script indicates that there is information available to tell us what to think about and what not to.

If I indicate that John went into a restaurant and ordered a hamburger, it is not necessary to reason that John orders a hamburger, the waitress knows that he wants a hamburger, and then try to figure out what she is going to do with that information. We know what she is going to do with that information; the question is: how do we know it? It isn't known as a natural consequence of ordering. Orders are in the MTRANS class. Every time someone gives an order, someone else doesn't simply execute it. Activity in our example is based on the waitress's role, the nature of a restaurant, and so forth. Consider another example. John went to a restaurant, he had some fish, he left a small tip. If I ask whether he paid for the meal, the answer is almost certainly yes. Did he enjoy the meal? Since he left a small tip, he may not have. Did he look at a menu? Probably. We have an intuition about such things; sometimes we have rather strong intuitions behind our interpretations. John went to a restaurant; he asked the waitress for some fish, and then he ate it. How did he get the fish? Obviously, the waitress brought it to him. We all know that; that is no problem. Scripts help answer the questions what did John eat, who served him, who prepared the meal? If I say John was served some fish but don't explicitly say he ate it, we still assume he ate the fish. All these assumptions have to be programmed into the machine; here is part of the restaurant script.

some roles and props: patron, waitress, food, menu, restaurant

ENTER: patron PTRANS patron to restaurant

SIT: patron PTRANS patron to table

ORDER: patron MTRANS food to waitress

SERVE: waitress PTRANS food to patron

EAT: patron INGEST food to patron

BRINGCHECK: waitress PTRANS check to patron

PAY: patron ATRANS money to restaurant

TIP: patron ATRANS money to waitress

LEAVE: patron PTRANS patron from restaurant

In brief, someone enters, sits down, orders, is served, eats, receives the check, pays, tips, and then leaves. The right side of the restaurant script shows how that information looks in the machine; it is the language of conceptual representation that I presented earlier with the MTRANS, the PTRANS, and PROPELs. What is literally shown is brief compared with what is actually necessary to write in a program; our knowledge about restaurants is enormous, it is not just those seven things. Now when I tell a story that includes something about entering, ordering, paying, and tipping, the listener can understand this because he can provide the appropriate context. Thus, it is not unreasonable to assume serving and eating and bringing a check; they aren't logical conclusions in any sense but somehow psychological. They represent things that are expected to happen; they are assumed. (See question 5 and responses.)

These kinds of assumptions are very useful. John went to Belmont, he enjoyed the activity, he left a tip with his friend. What kind of tip was it? The point is that even though I have been using the word *restaurant*, if one grasped the sentence at all, the word *racetrack* comes through strongly. Such words—like *racetrack*, or *restaurant*—suggest a whole special-purpose vocabulary. Thus, while we worry about this disambiguation problem in principle, in reality it barely exists. What happens is that highly ambiguous words like *tip* are constrained by the context to have very specific meanings. We don't have to think about the meaning of *tips*; we think about the meaning of *tip* that we are talking about. I have been discussing *ordering* all this time; no one is likely to start thinking that this was a sergeant ordering a private around, or somebody ordering something in a department store. One knew which sense of *order* it was and didn't have to think about rejecting all the other senses. A number of language theories that don't take context into account have to worry about disambiguation, which isn't so great a problem as might be imagined.

In the mid-70s, following Margie, we wrote a program called SAM, which could read newspaper stories, and then produce summaries. This is a story that it read:

> Friday evening a car swerved off Route 69. The vehicle struck a tree. The passenger, a New Jersey man, was killed. David Hall, 27, was pronounced dead at the scene by Dr. Dana Blauchard, medical examiner. Frank Miller, 32, of 593 Foxon Rd., the driver, was taken to Milford Hospital by Flanagan Ambulance. He was treated and released. No charges were made. Patrolman Robert Onofrio investigated the accident.

This is the summary that SAM produced:

> An automobile hit a tree near highway 69 four days ago. David Hall,

age 27, residence in New Jersey, the passenger, died. Frank Miller, age 32, residence at 593 Foxon Road in New Haven, Connecticut, the driver, was slightly injured. The police department did not file charges.

The program SAM was able to produce summaries by applying a script; the example here made use of the vehicle accident script. SAM took the script that it expected and started putting in all the inferences that were likely to be true. Notice that the summary contains some things that weren't actually in the story. SAM doesn't read the story, then manipulate the words; it takes the words, turns them into a representation, and then reads out the representation. The program could write a long summary, with more than the information provided, or a short one. It could also provide a summary in Spanish or any other language it happened to know. Furthermore, the system could answer questions.

Was anyone killed?	Yes, David Hall.
Was anyone hurt?	Yes, Frank Miller was slightly injured.
Did Miller go to the hospital?	Yes, he was in the Milford Hospital.
How did Miller get to the hospital?	The Flanagan Ambulance Company took him to the Milford Hospital.

Now what happens if the original story doesn't directly answer these questions? For example, the news release doesn't specifically say that anyone was hurt, it says Frank Miller was slightly injured. *Slightly injured* is hurt, and that should be recognized. The news story doesn't say why Miller was hurt, but we know why, so the machine should know. It doesn't say how Miller got to the hospital, but we should be able to deduce it from the story. Before going any further, try to repeat the story verbatim without looking. It is not likely that anyone will be able to do so; however, it is quite likely that some of those questions can be answered. The story is not in our heads any longer, but the representation is. All our program does is obtain a representation; it does not look at the story after that. In fact, the story is discarded once the representation is generated. At this point, the computer cannot repeat the story any better than a human, but it can repeat the representation and continually generate paraphrases of the story (which may be different than the story itself).

Scripts are very nice; they do many useful things. But the world is far more complex than racetracks and restaurants. For example, someone may wish to be mayor or someone may love Mary or hate her. Once certain wants or desires are expressed, human beings have the special ability to figure out what other actions might be expected. When we say "John wanted to be mayor; he got the arsenic," a diabolical plan suddenly emerges in the mind of the reader. *John loved Mary; he saw a large truck coming toward her; he gave her a shove.* Contrast that sentence with *John hated Mary; he saw a large truck coming toward her; he gave her a shove.* Now, I ask in each case, shoved her in which direction? It is not difficult for us to decide; the question is how, and the answer is goals and plans that realize those goals. (See question 7 and responses.) In general, people have a clear understanding of what is needed to accomplish some particular goal. In order to ask the computer to do this, we have to put into the machine a whole series of things related to understanding what a goal is and how to accomplish some particular plan to achieve the desired goal.

PAM was a program that didn't use scripts but only plans and goals. PAM read the following story:

> John wanted money. He got a gun and walked to the liquor store. He told the owner he wanted some money. The owner gave John the money. John left.

Now, if we ask why John got a gun, the machine will respond, "Because John wanted to rob the liquor store." Note that nowhere in the story is this explicitly stated. How did the program figure it out? There is a procedure for tracking goals and plans here. In effect, the story said that John wanted money and he got a gun. The machine must recognize that a gun is a threatening instrument. Threatening is a plan which the machine can deal with. The gun is also an instrument for overpowering. That too, is a plan which is part of the machine's repertoire; that plan is related to gaining control over things; in John's case, money.

John enters a liquor store. A liquor store sells liquor, but John wants money; does the liquor store have money? Yes, money is part of the nature of business. The program can go through this kind of reasoning to the point of figuring out what is going on. If we now ask why John had to threaten the shopkeeper, we would expect the program to be aware of the threatening nature of the situation even though no one was threatened explicitly. The program has to figure out the concept of threatening to understand the use of the gun, and so would anyone else. Why did John leave? He didn't want to be caught; this is obvious to humans; so the program had better know it, too. In fact, it is necessary to understand both the goals that have been explicitly stated as well as those that would likely exist now, given what has just transpired. The program must figure out goals and goals arising from goals. It is a complicated situtation.

This program can paraphrase from various points of view. For example, John would see the situation as follows:

> I needed to get myself some dough. So I got myself this gun and walked down to the liquor store, told the shopkeeper that if he didn't let me have the money, then I would shoot him, so he handed it over. Then I left.

The program PAM produced this paraphrase simply by reading the original representation that it had constructed and then assumed it was John. In order for the program to assume it was John, it had to know what plans and goals John had and what methods he used to carry them out. The program then went through the appropriate generation process. To present the owner's viewpoint, all PAM did was reverse roles.

> I was minding the store when a man entered. He threatened me with a gun and demanded all the cash receipts. Well, I didn't want to get hurt, so I gave him the money. Then he escaped.

This is the same story and the same information from the machine. Nothing has changed except one little node inside the machine that said focus on the owner.

In general, the problem is trying to figure out what people do, why they do it, and what their intentions are. We have actually tried to trick the program; for example, we gave it this story:

> John needed money. He got his gun and went into a liquor store. He offered to sell the gun to the store owner.

The program responded, "Ha, ha, I thought he was going to rob the store and he didn't. Boy, was I fooled." Now, I want to argue, of course, that is just what should have happened. PAM should be leaping to conclusions and sometimes making mistakes. For example:

> John took a gun and told the store owner he wanted money, and then the owner offered to write him a check.

Our expectations of what the owner is going to do have been violated. Many aspects of these situations are humorous, and it is important to understand why such things seem funny. One reason is that something happened that was unexpected, which is what we call an expectation failure. Each of the previously mentioned cases illustrates expectation failure. The machine must be made to expect things. A complicated model has been devised that permits the machine to say that it is ready for this or that now. When the situation does turn out as expected, then the program understands the story. When the situation is otherwise, the program creates an expectation failure.

People are reminded of past experiences all the time. I was concerned some time ago because programs were not being reminded. Consequently, at present we are changing the whole notion of machine memory so that it is constructed around expectation failures. If the machine had had a previous expectation failure, it would be reminded of it. Our programs will be reminded of other stories that they processed. In fact, if the program is told something like this, not liquor, not John, just someone looking as though he were going to rob someone else but didn't, the machine may be reminded of John and the liquor store and then tell a funny story. The reason for doing this is, of course, that we learn by modifying structures on the basis of expectation failure.

A set of actions, a set of goals, and plans to achieve them are specified for the system. The goal in this case is DELTA CONTROL, a desire for change in who controls some object, which, in the previous case, would be money. Each kind of goal has certain ways in which it can be attained. This collection of plans is called a planbox. A DELTA-CONTROL goal can be attained by eight methods; they are: ask, invoke theme, inform reason, bargain object, bargain favor, threaten, overpower, and steal. Using planboxes, a person's actions can be related to the person's goal; for example:

goal: John wanted Mary to give him some money.

ask: John asked Mary to lend him some money.

invoke theme: He reminded her of what good friends they were.

inform reason: He told her he needed to buy a present for his mother.

bargain object: He offered her a box of candy.

bargain favor: He told her he would repair her roof.

threaten: He threatened to ruin her reputation.

overpower: He locked her in the basement.

steal: He broke open her piggy bank and ran out of the house.

Consider the following problem: I have a desirable object *Y* that *X* covets; what should *X* do to obtain *Y*? He would have to select a method from the nine previously given. *X* might not think of obtaining the goal following the precise order specified, but ultimately this set would emerge. The set is ordered, and as human beings, we know not to begin with the last item on the list; instead, we start with the first one. The following sequence would not make much sense: First *X* says, "I would like object *Y* and if you don't give it to me, I will punch you in the mouth." I say no, and then *X* says, "Well, can I have it?" However, it could happen the other way around, starting with, "I would like the eraser. No? Then, I am going to punch you in the mouth unless you give it to me," which is acceptable.

All these programs have a certain modularity. The operations are done in sequence: analyze the sentence, make some inferences, apply a script, and finally apply plans. Despite the success that we have had, that procedure is wrong, and it took us a while to realize this. The major problem is that the flow of information is unidirectional; that is, inferencing, script application, and plan application cannot direct the parsing process when implemented modularly. In the pair of sentences *Bill gave John some very sound advice. He took it*, the program may start to think about the wrong sense of the word *take*. How can this be constrained? If the parsing program doing the analysis and generating meaning for the sentence, knows what else has gone before it, then it has the knowledge that is being activated, and it can derive the appropriate sense of the word. Before, we simply took our language and transformed it into meaning representations of the kind I have shown. We are now going through a radical revising effort in an attempt to have programs directed by higher level knowledge sources, such as scripts and plans; we are changing the modularity. What does this indicate about language analysis? It indicates that it cannot be done in the absence of knowledge. Any theory of language that doesn't include the theory of how knowledge directs language is not going to work.

As a test of our progress, not only do we try to understand stories, we sometimes try to have a computer make them up. The program Talespin is operated by creating a character and generating some plans and goals for him. The program provides a setting for the plot to develop, then attempts to attain the specified goals, and relates events as they occur.

> Choose any of the following characters for the story: bear, bee, boy, girl, fox, crow, ant, hen, lion, dog, wolf, mouse, goat, canary
>
> (bear, bee, boy, canary)
>
> (creating John bear)
>
> (creating a new cave)
>
> (creating a new mountain)
>
> John bear is at cave.
>
> (creating Irving bee)

(creating Sam Adams)

(creating Wilma Canary)

Choose any of the following miscellaneous items: berries, flowers, river, worm

(berries, worm)

Once the program is in an interactive mode, it produces a set of characters to choose from. Once we choose a bear, the program puts the bear in a cave because it has to have a place to live; creates a forest for the bear; provides mountains to climb, trees, honey, and other necessary things. Then the program asks for other characters and provides props; finally, it asks a few questions, who knows about the worm? In order to begin a story, the program has to know who knows what. The program then starts with the character's problems and how he attempts to solve them, and so forth. If one of the characters knows that a worm can be found in a patch of ground, that information can be used to bargain for something else that he may prefer. For example, the information is useful if a bird knows where some honey is but doesn't know where any worms are. Given a certain framework then, the machine is able to make up a story even though it may not be very interesting. What is interesting, and something that people never do, is to generate situations with major flaws. Let us consider a few examples where things don't work.

> One day Joe Bear was hungry. He asked his friend Irving where some honey was. Irving told him there was a beehive in the oak tree. Joe walked to the oak tree; he ate the beehive.

This was one of the stories generated by an early version of the program; what happened? There is a loop to change the program, based on changing the theory, based on what went wrong; that is precisely what is being done here. Why did Joe Bear threaten to hit Irving Bird? Joe didn't understand that when we are told something, then we know it; this seems obvious, but we forgot to put it in the program.

> One day Joe Bear was hungry. He asked his friend Irving where some honey was. Irving told him there was a beehive in the oak tree. Joe walked to the oak tree; he ate the beehive.

Here, we misrepresented honey and beehives so that the distinction between the contained and the container was not clear. It's like getting a can of tuna fish and eating the whole thing. When I say I'm going to get a can of tuna fish one would infer that I was going to open it. One has to tell the machine things like that.

> Henry Ant was thirsty. He walked over to the river bank where his good friend Bill Bird was sitting. Henry slipped and fell into the river. He was unable to call for help. He drowned.

This is not an unreasonable story; it just isn't the one the program was supposed to tell. The program includes many rules about things; for example, the consequences of initiating some act. The ant was supposed to be saved, but once the act of falling into the river occurred, the program didn't know how to save him.

> Henry Ant was thirsty. He walked over to the river bank where his good friend Bill Bird was sitting. Henry slipped and fell into the river. Gravity drowned.

A representation of someone falling into the river happens to be, recalling the mechanisms mentioned earlier, an example of PROPEL or, more specifically, pull. If gravity pulls someone into the river, isn't gravity in the river too? Anything that is in the river (unless it is a fish) but cannot get out, will drown. Henry Ant got out; gravity did not, so gravity drowned. By the way, this program eventually did generate *Aesop's Fables*. At this stage, it was still trying:

> Once upon a time, there was a dishonest fox and a vain crow. One day, the crow was sitting in his tree holding a piece of cheese in his mouth. He noticed that he was holding the piece of cheese. He became hungry and swallowed the cheese. The fox walked over to the crow. The end.

Now, we were trying to set up a standard fox and crow tale, but that cannot be done unless we have characters with realistic goals that they are able to act on. Animals are always hungry in our system. In this case, the crow was hungry and found some cheese in his mouth. Rather than using it to bargain with, he ate it; consequently, there was no story to tell. That, too, was fixed.

> Joe Bear was hungry. He asked Irving Bird where the honey was. Irving refused to tell him, so Joe offered to bring him a worm if he would tell him where some honey was. Irving agreed. But Joe did not know where any worms were, so he asked Irving, who refused to say. Joe offered to bring him a worm if he would tell him where a worm was. Irving agreed, but Joe did not know where any worms were, so he . . .

This is called an infinite loop in computer programming; some global fixes are needed.

> One day, Henry Crow sat in his tree holding a piece of cheese in his mouth. Up went Bill Fox. Bill saw the cheese and was hungry. [Hunger is now added to his goal stack, which is generated by the program but will give us an idea of what is actually done.] He said, "Henry, I like your singing very much, won't you please sing for me?" Henry, flattered by this compliment, began to sing. The cheese fell to the ground. [Wasn't that what was intended?] Bill Fox saw the cheese on the ground, and was very hungry. [Hunger is now added to his goal stack again.] He became ill. [Ill because he had been so hungry. If you are very hungry, you become ill. We were carried away there.] Henry Crow saw the cheese on the ground. He became hungry, but he knew that he owned the cheese. He felt pretty honest with himself, so he decided not to trick himself into giving up the cheese. He wasn't trying to deceive himself, either, nor did he feel competitive with himself. But he did dominate himself [these are all the things we have to go through when selecting a plan] and was very familiar with himself, so he asked himself for the cheese. He trusted himself, but he remembered that he was also in a position of dominance over himself, so he refused to give himself the cheese. He couldn't think of a good reason why he should give himself the cheese. [If he did, he would lose the cheese.] So, he offered to get himself a worm, if he would give himself the cheese. That sounded okay but he didn't know where any worms were. So he said to himself, "Henry, do you know where any worms are?" But, of course, he didn't, and on and on and on.

The problems here are clear. We have to remember what has been put into the programs to make sure that the various items coalesce. If one permits incomplete planning, knowledge, and understanding of things, then what just happened can happen. That is, someone may see the owner of something he wants and discuss the object with the owner without ever realizing that he is, in fact, the owner.

> Once upon a time, there was a bear named Joe who lived in a cave in the mountain. One day, he was feeling hungry, so he went to his friend, Irving Bird. "Irving," he said, "Will you tell me where I can find some honey?" Now Irving liked Joe a little, but he wanted to play a trick on him. "Certainly; Arthur Bee has some over in his beehive in the oak tree." Irving was lying. There wasn't such a bee, although there was an oak tree.
>
> Joe, being an honest bear, decided to ask Arthur for the honey. "I guess he will like me enough to give me some honey," Joe thought. So he walked across the valley to the oak tree and lo and behold, no beehive. Joe was pretty mad at Irving for lying to him about Arthur. Joe decided Irving might tell him where Arthur really was if he brought him a worm. So he went back to Irving. "Say, Irving, would you tell me where Arthur is if I brought you a worm?" "Oh sure,"

> replied the bird. "Good!" thought the bear. He went off to get a worm he knew about. He brought it back and gave it to Irving. Irving was very hungry and ate the worm. "Dumb bear," he says to Joe. Joe was mad. He couldn't find out where Arthur was to ask him about the honey. "Ah, maybe he can bring the honey to me," he thought. He was still mad at Irving and knew he couldn't trust him or ask him to do a favor for free. He couldn't think of any good reason why Irving should help him, so he decided to offer him another worm. "Look, Irving, if I bring you another worm will you ask Arthur if he will bring me the honey?" "Of course." On and on and on and on.

This story continues for a long time. The point is, the dumb bear never learns, and the story never ends.

In general, then, the difficulty is trying to figure out what people really know. Once we were able to handle these simpler stories adequately, we started thinking about more difficult things, one of which was what an expert knows. Because real experts know too much boring detail, we selected experts from a different group, the U.S. Senate.

We decided to model a U.S. Senator, giving him two sets of ideologies to choose from, liberal or conservative; the one presented here is the conservative. The senator has a naïve view of the world—mainly, that the Soviets want to control the world, while the United States wants to save the world—and this is the context in which the program understands the data.

We entered such information as the fact that the U.S. Congress is expected to approve the Panama Canal Treaty. The program understands that sentence, recognizing that it is a parliamentary procedure script. There was a vote, a treaty was passed, and other details were included as well. The program begins by determining what is happening in terms of the goals it understands. In this case, it starts with the notion that the U.S. goal will be violated, because U.S. military strength will be decreased by this act. (We have to go through some reasoning to reach that conclusion.)

Once this step has been completed, the program is ready to understand anything we may ask. Should the United States approve the treaty? (By the way, all questions are in standard English, and the output appears as though it were typed on a typewriter.) The program knows the treaty is detrimental to the United States, because the United States will cede control of the canal to Panama, which is another way of saying that the United States will become weaker. What might happen if the United States loses the canal? Russia may try to control the canal—a logical inference from what happens anytime that the United States loses anything. Why would Russia try to take over the canal? Russia wants to expand its military controls; everyone knows that, and the

Panama Canal obviously has military value. In general, military value is the kind of thing the program understands. The program knows that Torrijos is a communist, so Torrijos will let Russia control Panama.

In terms of structure, the program has a set of trees that permits it to interpret and act from the viewpoint of a conservative. The program understands that, in order to contain communism, a U.S. conservative will have several subgoals; these include military aid and a strong military, which are of greater importance than the goal of human rights. In other words, given a set of choices, the program will always choose a military solution, such as increased military aid to a country that likes us, rather than encourage an improved human rights situation.

To enable the program to express itself on armaments, it was informed that the U.S. Congress had voted to fund the Trident submarine. Why did the U.S. Congress do this? The U.S. Congress wants the U.S. armed forces to be stronger; that seems obvious enough. However, the program now goes through what's called a set of counterplanning strategies. If some particular event doesn't happen the way it should from the conservative point of view, what can be done to change it? To cope with contingencies, the program must know how to block and unblock goals. When faced with an increase in the number of Russian nuclear submarines, the program can respond in several ways. It may assume that the construction of more nuclear submarines will make Russia stronger, and if Russia becomes stronger, we will have to become stronger. The conclusion is that the United States should build more submarines; however, not all goals or choices are so obvious. Why should we be paying for the eventuality that *X* may try to block *G*? What procedures should be followed to prevent the goal blockage? When many goals are threatened, what schedule of priorities should be followed? The program must be able to answer these questions.

As I am sure the reader realizes, an interesting transformation has taken place. Initially, the problem was one of language; the effort was directed toward computer programs that could understand language. Now all of a sudden, the struggle is with counterplanning strategies. If we ask if that is language, the response is, it is or it isn't, depending on how we wish to define the domain of language. Perhaps, too, there are larger questions here, more important than language itself. If we want to build an intelligent computer, the computer must have the kinds of information we have. However, it is of no value to introduce information in encyclopedic form; what is in an encyclopedia is not the interesting part of what we know. What is of interest is the nature of an intelligent human's response in situation *A* when *B* occurs.

While it may seem odd that this work should be carried out in the language section of a computer science department, let me point out that this is, in fact, what AI is all about. Minsky made a comment that no one in computer science likes the people in AI. I would like to point out two reasons why. One, AI gets all the publicity, and computer scientists don't like that. Second, the kinds of things being done in the AI camp are foreign to most computer scientists; I find this fact to be the more important one. It isn't obvious where AI fits into the general role of computer science.

Artificial intelligence is concerned with cognition. Calling the machines that we use *computers* is really a misnomer; from the AI point of view, they are *cognizers*. We are trying to formalize knowledge. Artificial intelligence is in the knowledge business, which doesn't mean that we don't wish to be practical. Every now and then, we would like to create something technologically innovative or even useful. Consequently, an attempt was made to grasp reality, satisfy the computer scientists, and satisfy the defense department. We wanted to create something in the information realm that they would actually be able to use. The problem is this: take the pertinent political information that comes over a news wire, summarize it, and remember it. FRUMP, which reads quickly, is the program that attempts this; SAM is not used, because it is slower and very careful. FRUMP is more careless than SAM but does read quickly. FRUMP knows about fifty or sixty different domains of knowledge; it ignores things it isn't looking for, that is, that don't fit into the domains. FRUMP can read stories from the UPI wire as they come in and from that produce a summary; FRUMP can be directed to become an expert on some particular individual or set of individuals.

> Secretary of State Edmund Muskie went on a plane from the United States to Europe today, Secretary of State Edmund Muskie talks with Carter during briefing, Secretary of State Edmund Muskie gave a speech to a group on Monday. [This generator was not so sophisticated as the preceding ones; we sometimes decrease in technology.] Secretary of State Edmund Muskie had a talk with Nader in Brussels on Monday.

FRUMP is trying to learn all there is to know about the secretary of state by reading every single story that comes over the news wire. The first program reads every story that it knows about, and the second continually attempts to update its information on the basis of what it learns at the point where it is building a data base. The second program is called CYRUS, because it was working on Cyrus Vance in the beginning (the name is also an acronym, Computerized Yale Reading and Understanding Service). We would like this program to be able to read the newspaper all day, every day, and then know everything. We would also like it to understand what it reads, make inferences, generalize across stories, and so on.

At present, we can converse with the program that has been reading about Cyrus Vance and Edmund Muskie, and it will answer questions as if it were one of these gentlemen. For example, if we ask, "Where are you today?" Cyrus may answer, "In the United States." This implies that there haven't been any travel-related stories recently, and we would assume that if he had been away, he came back. "Where were you three weeks ago? Why did you go to talk with Andrei Gromyko? Whom did you talk with at NATO headquarters in Brussels?" These are the kinds of questions that can be handled. "Did you give a speech?" "Yes, to a group of reporters at NATO." "When was the last time you were in Egypt?" This is an entirely different subject but not an inappropriate question, since the machine doesn't forget. The response is September 1978. "Why did you go there?" "To negotiate the Camp David Accords." "Whom did you talk with there?" "With Anwar Sadat about the Camp David Accords."

While these questions are not all that easy, consider a still more difficult question: "Has your wife ever met Mrs. Begin?" Now, Cyrus Vance would know that,. and any program reading every story about Cyrus Vance should also know that. How would a reader of the same stories be able to answer this one? Well, the real Cyrus Vance's reasoning might go something like . . . I certainly attended social functions with Mr. Begin. I've also taken my wife to some of them. Mrs. Begin attended some of them. The question is, did they in fact attend a function at the same time. First he would try to remember a specific trip. It would have been either a trip to Israel or when the Begins visited Washington. "Have I taken my wife to Israel? Yes. What did we do when we went there? We went to the hotel, took a nap, and later that evening, we did go to a party. Who was at the party? I remember that we toasted each other and had dinner and Begin was there. He was the host. Was his wife there? Yes, I believe she was. Well, they must have met then."

There is no direct route to the answer, and the program isn't trying to sort or match words to things; it is going through a process that permits it to answer the question. Information is not sorted and stored in categories. If we ask, "What heads of state have you met?" the program will only be able to determine which heads of state it has met in terms of situations. There is no heads-of-state category that lists them all. That would make the answer to this particular question easier, but in general people do not construct their memories in such a way—nor does our program. It does remember places. It remembers all the trips. Thus a search might scan each trip looking for the pertinent details.

If computers can keep track of the political news, perhaps they should be able to argue as well. Imagine the following conversation between a husband and wife:

> Where were you last night? [The husband had come home late.] I went bowling with the boys. I thought you hated bowling? It's okay when I have some company. Aren't I company? It's not the same.

Many of us have had that kind of argument in one form or another. The question is how to develop a computer program that can have that kind of a conversation. Getting into a fight with a computer program may seem a bit silly, but, it is very important to have that capability. Remember, the goal is to create programs that simulate human activity as closely as possible. People communicate on many levels at once, and have to be able to deal with both literal and nonliteral meanings. In fact, if we want to communicate with someone, we have to analyze the intent of everything that is said on every level we know about, and analyzing emotional intent is not different from analyzing intent from some other perspective.

We are interested in figuring out what is going on in a conversation. We might call the last example an automated lie detector—the program is trying to figure out if someone is telling the truth; that is the primary goal. In the meantime, the program is, in effect, asking how does he feel about me? Does he still love me? Real-life conversations are actually like that; people are deeply concerned about what someone else thinks of them. Questions such as, is it possible he is not telling me the truth or how should I express what I want to say without offending him, given the appropriate context are the things that we really worry about when we talk. When one wants to get a computer program to talk, and does not take these aspects of human nature into account then there will be trouble. It is necessary to have computer understanding occur on multiple levels simultaneously. The program is always asking itself the question, what does it know, and what does it want to know. When it needs to know something, it will ask. It also wants to know what the person with whom it will interact knows. If the program talks to some person and doesn't know what that person knows, it's going to have a lot of trouble talking to him.

When someone comes up and asks me a question, I need to know whether he is my graduate student or a freshman in college or whatever because I'm going to treat him differently. The content of my response will be quite different. A program, as well, ought to know something about my own emotions and how I'm feeling. Humans need to know something about each other's feelings. I want to know something about what, or how much I believe what you are saying. I want to know something about our relationship. I want to know something about what I think you believe, what I believe and what you think I believe. I also want to know what my attitude is toward you and what your attitude is toward me and so on. Now those are not just things I'm checking. If I were it would be easy. Those are potential ways of responding. For any given sentence I can say it in at least twelve different ways. I can say the same thing at an emotional level or at some form of belief level. Sometimes one can combine them. The best sentences are the ones that combine all the possible levels at once.

So, here when we say I went bowling with the boys, the response is, well, let's see, how does that relate to my knowledge to date? These are the things that I know about him. How do they relate to the knowledge that I needed to know? Depending on what she knew, the statement may or may not have satisfied her. The end of the conversation could have occurred right there. Where were you last night? I went bowling with the boys. END. She wanted to know it and now she knows it. But if we are going to have more levels and more goals than that, tracking through a conversation, that would not be the end. If at the trust level it says, that doesn't sound true, or if at the relationship level it says, if he's going bowling with the boys, he is not spending time with me, then I'm offended. Each one of these levels deals with something that I know about him. One level would indicate he doesn't like bowling, so why would he do something he doesn't like? Another might treat attitudes and their expression. I may have an attitude that I don't wish to project. I'm feeling mad, but I don't want to say that I'm feeling mad. The whole problem of analyzing something and then responding to it can become extremely complicated.

At the present time, we are trying to program machines to respond in a number of new ways. First, it would be rewarding to have a machine understand the full emotional import and effect of what is going on around it. A second desirable feature would be the ability to figure out what might be happening when it is not kept completely up to date; it should do this on the basis of what it had been told on previous occasions.

We have a program that has been monitoring UPI wires solely for stories about terrorism, with the intent of making the machine an expert on terrorism. The program does have some capability in this second area. One of the items that this program noted early in its developing expertise was that if it weren't told who the protagonist was in an act of terrorism in Ireland, the program could assume it was the IRA. This doesn't seem very significant, but the machine reached the conclusion itself. Furthermore, it did make some leaps that were slightly more profound. For example, if it weren't told who was the target of a kidnapping in Italy, it would assume it was a businessman, because most of the time it was. Furthermore, if it weren't told the weapon in New Zealand, it would infer a boomerang. I was a bit skeptical of this last conclusion, so I checked. When I checked what the program had read, I found that terrorists in New Zealand did tend to use boomerangs as their weapons. Now, the program made a lot of dumb inferences, too. It concluded, for example, that bombs in El Salvador never explode, because it had read five or six stories about El Salvador where bombs were planted but no one was injured. Since then, the program has received additional information and changed its "mind". The program may leap to conclusions, but it is ready to reformulate them, should the need arise.

Each one of the programs that I discussed has certain attributes. Now we are trying to outfit our machine with a memory. The major emphasis is not language per se. The problem of *language* in a sense is a misnomer. The major thing we work on is useful memory; memory such as we have. We are trying to develop computer program memories by having the programs store the representation of a story, pick the next story, and use a previous story to help interpret it. We no longer have scripts; instead, we have procedures that read stories. Every time something doesn't go according to plan, the machine tries to figure out why. When it does figure out why, it stores that information in the category of expectation failures. It then uses that expectation failure and attempts to explain it.

Consider this scenario. When little Johnny enters a restaurant for the first time and orders something, he gets it. He thinks to himself, "This lady will do anything I want." So he shouts, "Get me the catsup!" She doesn't bring it; furthermore, she becomes angry with him. Johnny should then consider why his expectation was not fulfilled. We want Johnny to remember that expectation failure, but if that is all he does, he is in trouble. He is not going to learn; he must make sense of his expectation failure. Luckily, Johnny is likely to have a parent who will explain that he cannot speak rudely to waitresses and expect them to respond favorably. Johnny will store that expectation-failure explanation which says, one can ask, but one shouldn't be nasty, inside his restaurant script. Once that concept is stored, if he is nasty again, or if he hears someone else being nasty, he will say, that reminds me of the time that I was nasty and it didn't work. Gradually, he will accumulate a whole memory in terms of that script. When we start out, we have scripts that are full of standard normalizations but do not remember anything in terms of memory or expectation failures; as experiences occur, normal memories develop. An example of how this works follows.

We give our program a restaurant script and then send it to Burger King; it has never been there before. Nothing goes according to plan: We are supposed to sit down, but that isn't possible. First, we have to stand in line. Someone is supposed to come over to us to take our order, but, it turns out that we have to go over to someone and give him the order. There is no menu to look at, and, worst of all, we have to pay for the food before receiving it. Then we have to take it to our table and finally sit down. In Burger King, the sequence of all these things is contrary to past experience; this fact is stored as an expectation failure.

Now, we send the program to McDonald's, where we hope it will immediately say, if it is an intelligent computer, "This reminds me of Burger King." Now, why should it be reminded of Burger King? Because the same expectations are failing again; when expectations fail twice in a row, the second should remind us of the one that was stored previously. The experience of being reminded should cause the learner to make a new generalization; that is, if the learner is intelligent, he will construct another class of expectations.

We are no longer using scripts directly; we are creating knowledge structures that automatically modify themselves and create new ones. The current program for this process is called MOPS; it creates new scripts, new generalizations, over which we no longer have control. It says, "I don't know, this memory went this way, but based on a series of expectation failures, I am going to change the system, and move them that way." The terrorism program has begun to understand all sorts of things about terrorism that we don't know, because it is learning about terrorism and it is coming up with all sorts of generalizations that are true. Storing expectation failures when things don't work out quite right, generating new expectation systems, and learning from them again is the way to learn.

The interesting thing, of course, is at what level the storing is done. (While it may not be obvious to the reader why this is interesting, it probably is to someone in AI.) Recall when Johnny was rude to the waitress in the restaurant; she didn't give him what he wanted. Now, he could store that information as an expectation failure inside restaurant, but then he will behave rudely in a department store. We don't want him to do that; therefore, we want him to store his expectation failure inside something more general. Therefore, we have eliminated specific knowledge sources and created a more general knowledge source called ORDERING, which is used by restaurant. Restaurant is able to use ORDERING when it needs to order and is quite able to color ORDERING with things specific to restaurants, like menus. But when restaurant receives expectation failures that are not specific—for example, how to speak to people—it stores that information in ORDER-

ING, and that same ordering procedure can be used by a department store. Thus, the program doesn't have to relearn how to behave in a new context; it can be reminded more generally.

Last, we are now working on a simpler problem, which I call the Romeo and Juliet problem. If you have seen the play *West Side Story*, it should remind you of Romeo and Juliet even though the context is not the same. It is New York, not fourteenth-century Italy; it is gang warfare, not family disputes. How does the human mind find what is (and is not) the same in these structures? The restaurant ordering approach is not going to work, because these two stories are quite different. On one level, however, they are almost identical; that level is called Mutual Goal Pursuit Against Outside Opposition. What one is doing is tracking goals and conditions that pertain to those goals.

What is the lesson of all this? Ultimately, it means that all the problems I have discussed are part of the larger problem of knowledge representation. If we want intelligent computers, we have to figure out the kinds of knowledge and memory structuring that exist in human beings for organizing and storing the information they receive. Once we discover that, presumably we can get machines to do it, too. When machines are so organized, they will start behaving just as intelligently as you and I. In fact, it shouldn't be too long before they are better than you and I, because machines will have a number of advantages that we lack. One is: they don't become bored.

3. *Questions And Replies*

MARVIN MINSKY AND ROGER C. SCHANK

Question 1: Do you regard Joseph Weisenbaum as a Luddite—akin to those English workmen who destroyed the looms as a protest?

Schank: I don't think Joseph Weisenbaum is destroying anything; I think he asks questions that are worth asking, but I have difficulties with his approach. For example, once I asked him what he meant when he said computers cannot understand. "What level of understanding are we talking about? Assume there are eight levels of understanding and level eight is the level where true human empathy of the kind found only in successful marriages occurs. Is that the kind of understanding you believe computers are incapable of?" He replied that it was. I agree with that, since I am not convinced that most people can understand at that level very well. I asked him why not say that computers cannot understand at the deepest level of empathetic understanding between two humans? They will not fall in love with each other or with us. But he hasn't done that; he prefers to say that computers cannot understand at all. I think that, in general, the questions he asks about computers and their social consequences and so on are worth asking, but there is something in this attitude that disturbs me.

Minsky: Yes, I see a very similar problem. If you look at Weisenbaum's book *Computer Power and Human Reason*, it is mostly "If someone is different from you, how can you trust that person?" There is nothing in his discussion that concerns computers. It is about what to do if someone else obtains power but that person doesn't have your interests at heart or doesn't understand them. Then he says the trouble with computers is that they are not likely to understand you, and, in fact, cannot possibly. That is another opinion and one in which he is not justified because, as Roger said, as we do more and more research on understanding how humans function, we will be able to program that understanding into computers. The main issue is how we can put a computer in charge of a situation. For example, Weisenbaum speaks of a juvenile court situation where there is a teenager who has done something illegal and the judge has to use his humanity to decide what to do with the teenager. The point is how can we trust a judge to make such a decision—and most of us don't.

Schank: I am fond of a response on a similar level to the issue of what would be the ultimate for computers. One of my fantasies is to elect a computer to be president. I mean that quite seriously in the following way: It would be a computer capable of doing what it were asked to do. It would be able to adjudicate a variety of situations. What we want is not elections of people, where we elect someone who looks nice and speaks well, but elections of beliefs, like our conservative senator. If there is going to be an election for anything, we should decide whether Russia has to be contained and how much, or whether welfare programs should be operating and for how much, and we should have votes on these issues. All the beliefs elected by the people would then be put inside the machine, which would operate according to them. We might not like what we get, but we would get what we asked for.

Question 2: Professor Minsky, you commented on the fact that in a sense AI has failed. It seems to be working backward from calculus to algebra and finally to stacking blocks.

Minsky: Because we have to understand understanding.

Question 3: When that is realized, how close are we to reverting to the approach that early workers in the field of AI had when they were working on cellular automata and trying to simulate the brain. Will the approach be in that direction, or will it be toward solving specific problems?

Minsky: The question is: Should we try to discover exactly how the brain works? I don't think so. I don't think anyone will understand how the brain works until AI has shown how the brain might work. I have very little faith that brain science will be able to deal with this machine. Presented with this gadget with billions of parts and very poor instruments for seeing what is in them, brain scientists do just what you and I and everyone else do—they try to use common sense on an extraordinarily complicated machine. Today there is no generally accepted theory of how memories are stored in the brain. There has been a theory—which is almost a hundred years old now—since synapses were discovered, that somehow memories are stored by altering the strength of connection between one nerve cell and another; but there is no accepted theory. It is very rare to find a science with perhaps a hundred thousand scientists and no principal paradigm in which they are working. Now, there are people working on chemicals, who know that when a certain chemical is administered, people generally react in a particular way; they also see certain cells metabolize faster than others. I am not saying there isn't a tremendous amount of knowledge. What I am saying is that the state of neuroscience is very weak because it doesn't have an idea about how knowledge is represented in the brain, and as far as I can tell, there hasn't been any progress since 1930 in neuroscience in this area. I think that we will be able to help them solve the problem. Frankly I don't think that a young person interested in understanding how the brain works should work on the brain now. He or she should work on AI for a few years.

Schank: An example of one of the problems in that area is split-brain research. Scientists have discovered that when they spoke to the left brain of a subject, the subject could respond, but when they spoke to the right brain, the subject couldn't. This is an over simplification, but it has led scientists to conclude that language is on the left side. But language consists of many parts, and it may be that the very last output mechanism is on the left; however, that would be the smallest tip of the language phenomenon. Brain scientists make statements about language, but when asked what they mean, their response is likely to be that they don't really know anything about language. You have to know what you are looking for when you look.

Question 4: What is the current state of the art of spoken word and sentence recognition?

Schank: There is a problem that, in principle, cannot be solved until all the problems I was discussing have been solved. Simply, there is no way of hearing speech if you don't understand it. For example, if I started to speak a foreign language that you didn't know, then asked you to list all the phonemes, you would have great difficulty. Spoken language is completely strung together, each thing slurred into the next. I skip over a variety of words. Your expectations about what I might be saying help fill in all that information. A computer attempting to understand the spoken word is like someone trying to understand a foreign language. It is difficult to figure out even what the rudimentary sounds are. We have to have expectations derived from our knowledge about language. When we have finished, I think that people working in speech recognition can seriously set to work. Right now, they are doing what I consider to be preliminary work, which may be of some use when the whole system has been put together.

Minsky: For fairly clearly spoken English, there are programs that do well in segmenting. For $50,000, there are machines that can be taught about two hundred words and pick them out of sentences with a fair degree of reliability. This area is developing. In fact, I think we should appreciate the last minutes of silence in our civilization because we are soon going to have machines understanding simple language. Appliances are already beginning to speak. One of my students just wrote a story about a household of the future where the vacuum cleaner complains to the toaster about getting crumbs on its floor.

Question 5: When you speak of trying to discover how human understanding and knowledge are developed, are you referring to how that process works in Indo-European thought processes? Do you think that there are cultural constraints that affect how we store and understand information? I know that this was the case in the Whorfian hypothesis, which has been discarded but is still very attractive and often used to explain male and female behavior. The idea is that men and women learn different grammatical constructions. Are your results constrained by a particular Western European culture, and might things be different in a different culture?

Schank: If you ask questions at that general level, you come up with things like the Whorfian hypothesis. If you ask questions at a very specific level, then you can come up with more treatable things. Consider, for example, a restaurant script; is a restaurant script likely to be used in Afghanistan? The answer is probably not; they would have different scripts. Do they have scripts is the second question you want to ask; that is, do they have standardized methods of doing things? Obviously they do. Every culture has standardized methods, but they are not identical. We have our plans and goals, and they have their goals and plans to achieve them. Are they the same plans and goals that we have? No.

There may be similarity in some of the data, and there certainly should be similarity in the structures. I don't see the phenomenon of having scripts, plans, and goals as even being particularly human. For example, I think that cats and dogs have scripts, plans, and goals—of a simple sort—but they have them. We observe babies learning scripts very early in life. Basic to the human species is a desire to see a repetition of patterns that have been encountered before. Since most of our work is based on that kind of thing, I don't think there is much cultural influence except in terms of the data.

Minsky: The Whorfian idea that the concepts we receive determine forever the way we understand other ones must be true, because the way we assimilate new things certainly depends on what we already know. But I would deemphazise differences between cultures myself, because I find that people I meet aren't so different. Scientists from various cultures seem rather similar to me. People from the same neighborhood who have different intellectual backgrounds seem strikingly different. I think that differences between individuals are greater than differences between cultures.

Question 6: People do irrational things. Does AI properly model the human thinking mechanisms by taking that into account?

Minsky: There was no discussion of rationality in either of our talks. I think both of us have the view that when you have a situation you look in memory and find things that it matches or reminds you of. You find differences and you find prohibitions and expectations.

Schank: The problem is defining rational and irrational, which we are not trying to do. Our machine will serve its goals, and we can find out why it did something in terms of its goals. When we say that human beings behave irrationally, we really mean that we disagree with their goal choices.

Question 7: You refer to goals, but I think that in the case of humans, quite often the goals are not really known.

Schank: We don't know what our higher level goals are; we know the lower level ones. I think it depends on what goals we are referring to. If we mean thirty-year goals, then no, of course, we don't know them. But then we don't even have to think about them much, so our programs don't either.

Minsky: That also brings up the self issue. What do you mean known? Known to whom? Certainly people don't know what is going on in their minds or they wouldn't produce such bad psychological theories. Why was it the twentieth century before someone like Freud pointed out that there are things in people's heads that they don't know about? Why is it that people have this illusion that they do know what they are doing? When you say the goals are known, it might be that to the programmer the goals are known in his program. But, in fact, we had a Ph.D. thesis by John Doyle on the issue of what it would take for a program to have access to its own goals. It's a very tricky problem, because it's very bad for a program to know its own goals if it subjects them to the same treatment as other problems. Suppose I ask you, "What's your goal?" You say, "Well, it's to do this." And I say, "Well, is that worthwhile?" Then you get into a vicious circle because how do you decide what's valuable without reference to a goal?

It is not clear that being conscious of goals is possible or meaningful in either a machine or a person. Maybe a wrong question to ask.

Question 8: Dr. Schank, do your computers programmed for expectation failures know what they are? Is it the same as the theory of negative knowledge? Can a machine produce new knowledge that it has not been given?

Schank: Yes, that is my point; I suspect it is also Marvin's point. What we argue is that people don't learn from success, they learn from failure and, in a sense, failure drives every learning experience we have. For example, the TAILSPIN program had some failures, but we fixed them, we didn't let the program fix them. But as we teach the program to fix its own failures, it will alter what it knows. As it begins to alter what it knows, we will have a program that is genuinely changing and learning. Our argument is that that is what people do.

Minsky: Incidentally, a whole generation of psychologists and educators was trained in the wake of Skinner's book, on the behavior of organisms. On the basis of experiments with pigeons, Skinner concluded that only success-oriented learning is effective and failure-oriented learning is not of great value. This led to a doctrine in psychology called behaviour modification, which is primarily a procedure by which people are rewarded for doing something correctly. This theory of psychology is the dominant form taught in schools of education, and because they are twenty years behind, so-called positive reinforcement theories are the dominant ideology among nonresearch psychologists of our time. This is a very serious social problem.

Question 9: To pursue that point just a little further, in the last century it was fashionable to be involved philology and linguistics. Apparently, that was old fashioned and died out; is that approach likely to be revived now? It seems to me that much of the work that you are doing suggests that a resurgence is very likely.

Schank: Most of our work flies in the face of linguistics. The average linguist in an academic department in the United States would argue that what I am doing is absolutely wrong. Linguists are trying to formalize language in the absence of knowledge, as if language were a formal system in its own right. This is in opposition to a system that relies on plans and goals and knowledge and context. There is no doubt that a lot of work on language has to be done in the area that we are exploring, and we will have difficulty finding a place to do it in the current environment. Linguistics departments do not tend to support our work, so, the answer is yes, but I don't see how it will happen given present situation.

Question 10: The contention may be that what we are seeing in linguistics departments now is a residual of what was there in the nineteenth century.

Schank: No, in the 50s and 60s, linguistics was dominated by Chomsky, which is totally wrong.

Minsky: In the 50s, the new linguistics resembled behaviorism. Skinnerism became dominant in most psychology departments; now, transformational grammar and related ideas are determining things in linguistics departments. Work on the meaning of words has to be done in computer science departments on the whole. There is a new branch of psychology called cognitive psychology, which tries to understand how knowledge is represented psychologically. However, I am afraid that we will have to wait another ten to twenty years for linguistics departments to outgrow their mathematics envy. You see, Chomsky and some colleagues actually proved theorems about certain pieces of algebra connected with their models of language. This so stunned the linguistic community, because it looked like physics, that those people became very powerful. It will take a while for the analysis of semantics and common sense in language to overcome this particular movement.

Question 11: I would like to ask Professor Minsky about chess-playing programs. To what extent do these programs learn and grow from their own experience?

Minsky: Chess programs just slipped out of the main stream of AI quite a while ago. The chess programs we hear about today are offshoots of work on game playing that was done in the late 50s and is completely out of the current research environment. These programs don't do much learning. Basically, I see this as a side activity of hobbyists with no scientific interest, because the programs no longer have interesting ideas.

Question 12: What are the possible effects of AI on our society, and how soon do you see those effects taking place?

Minsky: Not for quite some time. But it is important to note that AI research is often confused with advanced computer science because many of the same people are involved. For example, it was people in AI laboratories who, years ago, developed computer time-sharing advanced operating systems and the most advanced computer languages now being used. The flourishing of computer networks and other advances that exist on a large scale today are the effects of our tool building. In a sense, AI research is almost the same as advanced computer research. Information retrieval systems, found in office automation now, too, are the result of earlier research on how to store information in simple ways. There is a ten- or twenty-year lag before something going on now will be useful to the public.

Schank: Another problem that was alluded to earlier is the lack of manpower in AI; AI research is carried out in only a few laboratories with a few people. What we could do, for example, and without great effort, is put a program like the CY-FR program on home computers to enable people to read newspapers automatically. But we would need a developmental staff knowledgeable enough and willing to do that; we don't have that staff. Anyone who has been trained to do AI work would be reluctant to do that, because it is not particularly interesting. Researchers in AI consider themselves to be scientists and are more interested in discovering truths than in developing technology. We need a spin-off group who have learned AI technology and are prepared to implement it, and they don't exist yet.

Question 13: It has been pointed out that if a precise language-understanding system were possible, it could be used in a repressive way. For example, a government could automatically tap every telephone conversation in the country and monitor ones that were of interest. I wonder if that has any deterrent effect on you and your work?

Schank: Of course it disturbs me; but any technological innovation has the potential for misuse. The dilemma for every builder of technology is: should we stop expanding technology for this reason? My answer is no.

Minsky: In particular, politicians and not scientists should be held responsible for the consequences of technological discoveries. If you invent the gasoline engine, then you can make tanks that will drive over cities. Seriously, to even have the idea that people should consider not discovering things because they might be misused is in a sense betraying some very deep more important principles. The fact that people think they should address the scientist about his responsibility rather than think about the problem of why governments would be likely to repress, indicates to me that the West has already fallen. The fact that people are worried about learning the truth about the mind because it might be misused might be understandable. But surely we have already invented enough things, such as H-bombs, to be misused. It is governmental use—not the scientist's discoveries—that need attention.

Part II

Computer Influences in Modern Culture

Sticks and stones may well have been used for breaking bones by early man. However, when we consider the problems involved in using such tools as weapons to wound an antelope or a wildebeest, it may have been the ability of a group of hunters to communicate that hurt just as much as the weapons themselves. In the hunt, foresight, planning, coordination, cooperation, and communication are as essential as the weapons for a successful outcome. These tools are the same ones needed for problem solving in any sociopolitical situation. When a multipurpose tool, which has, for example, the ability to help plan, coordinate, and communicate, is added to the repertoire of tools that previously had served only immediate ends—such as bashing a neighbor's skull—then we gain the advantages of being better prepared, having a more smoothly operating team and being able to attain more complex goals.

Planning for and predicting the future has a checkered history. In the nineteenth century, Laplace expressed the opinion that if the positions and velocities of all the particles in the universe were known at some particular moment, then it would be possible to predict the future. Although no modern scientist would entertain such a deterministic clockwork view of the universe, the idea remains captivating. That is, the future is basically spelled out, and if we could only learn the code, the possibilities for exploiting that knowledge would be endless.

Some gamblers are confident that they can determine beforehand the outcome of an uncertain event—can predict, for example, the outcome of a race because they have a special understanding of "the track." Even in the face of continued loss, inveterate bettors will not admit that their system is wrong, only that they have failed to use it correctly; they have ignored certain bits of information that should have been included. While the addicted gambler must bet and then wait for the feedback (often painful but generally not interpreted as negative in his system), many politicians, for example, must also make an immediate decision in hope that it meshes with desirable future events—as well as with voters' sentiments in the next election.

Imagine the difficulties of city planners in Mexico City. Their job is to lay out a scenario (including, for example, housing, food and water supply, transportation, industrial growth, sanitation, air pollution, and crime) for the next several decades that will permit the city to function efficiently as it undergoes an enormous increase in population. Exacta wagering seems far simpler. Politicians desiring to make the best policy decision on some sensitive issue, executives of a large corporation considering a new marketing venture, a military staff attempting to anticipate the results of implementing a new weapons system, or a citizen wondering how the implementation of a new technology will affect his private life would all like a greater sense of certainty about the future than when they stand at the race track's two-dollar window.

A knowledge of possible scenarios of the future, each based on a different set of assumptions, would be of enormous value. If, for example, we were concerned about the future of the terrestrial ecosystem, it would not be difficult to conclude that the system is being subjected to a series of stresses unprecedented in its four-billion-plus-year history. Our ability to exploit the potential of available materials (especially the resource of energy) and our tendency toward rapid population increase have placed us in an extremely difficult position. Each acquisition of power that becomes an integral part of society is accompanied by a concomitantly increased vulnerability. Imagine the outrage if the electric utility companies were to say, "On vacation, no power this week." Count the number of lights, electric motors, heating elements, air conditioners, typewriters, computers, telephones, radios, and televisions that would be functionally useless. Or imagine a note saying, "The local water supply is contaminated, discontinue use", or another saying, "No more natural gas, fuel oil, coal, gasoline, or diesel fuel for at least six months." How long would food remain in the groceries? How long could we survive?

Societal needs and dependencies have induced change in the world order; some associated long-term effects are becoming manifest only very slowly. Undoubtedly, some strains may not yet be visible, but due to the effective inertia of the system, once the stresses have initiated some dynamic change, those changes are extremely difficult to reverse. Most often, hidden strains produce negative results, which the public confronts as a crisis requiring immediate attention. A short breeding cycle and modern transportation, for example, can be a bad combination: witness the appearance of the Mediterranean fruit fly in California.

The collective desire for certain goods or outcomes is affecting both the local and global natural order. Atmospheric pollutants, depletion and contamination of aquifers, and the extinction of various species are examples of the endangering side effects of attempting to fulfill certain desires. Each of these negative side effects is the result of a policy of short-term expediency or gain. Long-term outcomes have sometimes been clearly perceived yet blatantly ignored. The tobacco industry denies, no matter what evidence to the contrary, that the "localized pollution" of smoking cigarettes has a serious negative effect on the health of those who smoke. Most coal-burning operations are not interested in learning of distant problems of acid rain. Hooker Chemical apparently continued to dump known toxic wastes in Love Canal long after it was clear that there were real dangers. (Hooker then sold the contaminated land as building sites.) Beef fed with DES was banned from United States and Canadian markets, but sales continued elsewhere.

In other instances, long-term effects were simply not anticipated. Lack of knowledge of complex systems often does not make it possible to know in any detail how today's acts will affect our future. Many chemical-dumping sites were thought to be safe but over the long term proved to be dangerous. In many cases, toxic wastes did ultimately seep into the ground water. Independent of whether the difficulties which resulted were caused by gross negligence or lack of understanding or some combination of the two, some better way of taking long-term effects into account is needed. That one-third of all long-time workers dealing directly with asbestos, and their families died of a rare form of lung cancer; that the production of pesticides and herbicides caused severe and irreversible nerve damage resulting in the deaths of many employees; or that gas-powered heaters in some small cars gave off sufficiently high levels of carbon monoxide to cause severe and irreversible brain damage, are examples indicating the need for greatly improved planning and concern for long-term effects.

If we could build a representative model able to deal with some large-scale problem, simulate a variety of scenarios based on different policy decisions, then watch the dynamic developments, the influence on our decision making would be enormous. However, the gap between this fantasy and our present situation is indeed great. Constructing a model is one problem; constructing an accurate model is another. And the willingness to make a decision based on results from a model is yet another.

If a model is to represent accurately a "complex of events," for example, the escalation of a tactical nuclear exchange to a strategic one, then the model must include elements basic to the dynamics of that situation. The need to be complete without creating an overwhelming list results in an uneasy balancing act. (Even if we weren't trying to limit the list, the problem of including all necessary items is difficult, especially when the situation is unknown.) Once the list exists, the modeler must then be able to specify what the nature of the interaction between various elements should be. For example, if Russian tanks overwhelm NATO forces and begin an advance into Germany, what level of NATO tactical-nuclear weapons' activation will indicate a firm but limited response rather than a full-scale unleashing of the entire armory, and how will the Warsaw Pact nations respond? In the model (the Rand Corporation notwithstanding), what mathematical expressions, if any, should represent that interplay?

Of course, there may never be a one-to-one correspondence between a model created to describe a sociopolitical situation and reality. Given that a particular model is imperfect, the extent to which the outcome will be believed gives pause for reflection. Most political decision makers know nothing about the details of model building. Thus, another facet of the overall problem emerges: the relationship between the modeler and the person who must use the results. The problems of belief, bias, and vested interests in modeling cannot be ignored. Models of socio-political situations are not value free; they are not simply objective statements woven together. (Models in the natural sciences, while not ideal either, generally suffer less from these deficiencies.) Despite all reservations, models are still a valuable means of anticipating outcomes resulting from various choices.

With guarded optimism, careful thought, and effective communication, it may be possible to make good social and political choices. It is all too clear that in many cases of conflicting interests, armies stand ready to carry out politics by other means, as Clausewitz so antiseptically put it, should their side's desired goals not be attained through bargaining. We have learned little about how to avoid such conflict, but we do know that public and private discussions have great potential benefit. The mutual exploitation of power between computer and communication systems may be a key element in the decision-making process whether the problem is an internal corporate matter, a local political problem, or an international crisis.

Of course, all this may not matter very much if global stability is upended. The computer is a tool of such versatility that while it may be used to better mankind by assisting in communication and planning, it can also be used to further the aims of the military, should they be called on to act as arbiters. If computers can be used to give one side an advantage, be it in data reduction or "smart" artillery, the result is a shift in strength from a previous state and is potentially a destabilizing one. If the systems are in a complex yet effectively primitive state, reliability may be decreased even though the use of modern methods may have increased. One early news report on the Israeli invasion of Lebanon indicated that Syrian missiles had been rendered useless when the Israeli airforce knocked out a missile-control center. If such a report were true, it would be a clear example of the complexity/reliability problem. Uncertainty does not necessarily further stability.

It is ironic that the tool supposed to help find a stable solution can be, under some circumstances, destabilizing. Although we may be preoccupied with surviving the problems of resource allocation and global stability, the integrity of the individual must be kept clearly in view. It would make no sense to wait until all these problems were solved before worrying about the needs and the status of the individual. In fact, an acceptable solution to these problems must be sought in terms of the rights of the individual. While the computer may assist us in our daily lives, we must be sufficiently realistic to admit that however useful, these machines are unlikely to simplify our lives. Yet, on the other hand, we must be sufficiently vigilant to ensure that computers are not used to stifle or limit our freedom.

D. D.

4. *Models, Simulation, and System Dynamics*

DAVID F. ANDERSEN

To focus on the subject of this chapter, let me indicate two things that system dynamicists (people who build simulation models of public policy issues) don't do. Although system dynamicists know about computers and use them, they are not computer scientists. And although they know something about social science, they don't consider themselves to be social scientists in the conventional sense of the word. In fact, they are a class of researchers and analysts who are very interested in social problems and social policy and want to use the tools of social science and computers to help solve those problems or improve social responses to some of those problems.

The main theme of this chapter is what computers can contribute to the study of social problems. I would like to suggest that the advent of high-speed and inexpensive computing adds a new dimension—which I will call design—to the social-policy process. A word or two more about the concept of design may be useful at this point.

The physical and social sciences are involved, to a certain degree, in an atomistic process. That is, traditionally scientists of both sorts take naturally or socially occurring phenomena and divide them into smaller and smaller pieces. If we read any Ph.D. dissertation in either the physical or social sciences, we note that it is devoted to some highly specialized problem.

However, there are some people in the physical sciences who are no longer concerned with exploring finer and more increasingly minute problems; instead, they are interested in putting things back together and making them work. Those people are engineers. The thing that in my mind distinguishes engineers from practitioners in many branches of the physical sciences is that engineers are involved with design. They take small pieces of existing knowledge and put them together, creating new things.

We have a similar situation in the social sciences. However, a very different process must be involved whereby social scientists take those fragments of knowledge and combine them in a design process; I will discuss how computers help in the design of process for social policy.

SOCIAL POLICY PROBLEMS

Problems involving dynamic systems are closely related to the field of cybernetics. In describing the class of problems associated with this concept, let us start with something that doesn't look like a social problem at all—the airborne-fire-control problem. During World War II, a very real problem confronted the U.S. Navy and Air Force. Our forces were being attacked by enemy aircraft, and we had to direct our weapons to destroy those aircraft. However, human beings are not very good at directing guns at flying airplanes that are able to move very fast and dodge unpredictably. To assist in solving this problem, a formal mathematical theory—feedback theory—was developed, refined, and applied. Feedback theory deals broadly with processes controlling and stabilizing all types of systems that vary through time, such as moving aircraft. The solution was implemented using an early version of today's computers to help with the fire-control problem. In fact, primitive analogue computers were put on board most U.S. Navy destroyers and battleships to help direct antiaircraft fire against foreign aircraft.

After the war, that same body of theory was used in business administration schools to study a wide variety of problems, such as stability and employment processes within single firms. Analysts then began to ask numerous questions, such as how a corporation grows or declines or how various sectors of a firm work together to form a system of components. It wasn't long before system dynamicists became bolder and began to attack even broader problems: Why do urban areas grow and decline? What kinds of policies could revive urban areas? Most recently, system dynamicists are combining their knowledge of computers with their understanding of feedback systems to attack such problems as U.S. energy self-sufficiency, unemployment, and inflation.

All of these problems have some common characteristics; they are complex, dynamic, and feedback-driven. By complex, I mean that a large number of components interact—a very large number all of whose interactions must be considered simultaneously. By dynamic, I mean that these problems involve changes over time. Systems generating these problems involve large numbers of components that are all moving—imagine one or two hundred components all of which are changing and shifting at the same time. Finally, these changes are driven by feedback, which means that when we change something in the system right now, it will cause something to change that will cause something else to change, that will cause something else to change, that will eventually feed back to alter the initial situation.

THE NEED TO LINK HUMAN THOUGHT AND COMPUTER CAPABILITIES

When social systems exhibit problems that are complex, dynamic, and feedback-driven, the human mind finds it difficult to think about such problems. There are simply too many factors changing simultaneously for the human mind to grasp fully.

Consider the fact that as everyone knows, the price of gasoline at the pump is rapidly rising; let us approach that price increase as a problem. What is required to understand this problem is quite different from that required to comprehend DNA reproduction within a cell. It is very different, because the answer to why the price of gasoline is rising at the pump is available to the collective body of human knowledge. On the other hand, the collective body of human knowledge does not know why DNA molecules function as they do. Social problems are essentially different from those in the physical sciences. For example, if one were to collect the entire body of human knowledge, one would probably know why gas prices go up. If we could somehow have a massive research effort, we could conceivably know about all the processes that cause gasoline prices to increase precisely because those changes are the result of human actions.

However, the problem of organizing our knowledge about gas prices is complex; consider all the individual actions involving people in Iran, in shipping companies, executives in oil companies, and individual distributors. If we could somehow pull together all of that knowledge, it seems clear that those are the people who have made the decisions that have led to the rising prices. The problem is that if we did go through that exercise of interviewing those thousands of people and obtained all of the necessary information, we wouldn't know what to do with it. We would have such wealth of information that it would be difficult for any single mind to digest.

I propose that we use the computer to augment the ability of individual analysts to think about complex problems. Specifically, we will attempt to couple some properties that the human mind seems to be quite good at with those computer properties that complement the strengths of the human mind. Understanding one or two relationships at a time is an area where human minds excel. Our minds also have an uncanny ability to intuit relationships as well as design and create new solutions.

On the other hand, we want a computing machine to do what the human mind does not do so well; we want a very accurate bookkeeper. We want something to keep track of all the relationships that we understand and posit; something that is very much more precise than our minds are likely to be. It should never forget a relationship, and if we give it 500 relationships, it must remember all 500 relationships and unfold them exactly and precisely as the system of relationships evolves over a 50- , 100- , or 200-year period. That is something a human being might be able to do, but it would take months of effort.

By having the machine take over the bookkeeping functions, the social policy analysts can spend their time at system conceptualization and system design. I propose that we use the machine as a tool to augment or expand our ability to understand social problems by becoming a partner of human intuition and understanding.

THE CONCEPT OF A COMPUTER MODEL

Exactly how are computers going to help us understand problems better? The process is to design models—simulation models. A model is a small version of something that can be constructed and manipulated in a controlled situation. One can pick up a model, turn it around and look at it, and ultimately figure out how it works.

Scale models are very important, for example, in aerodynamics, where testing various models of wings in a wind tunnel is quite common. There are other kinds of models besides physical scale models. When we think about an urban area or unemployment, we don't know absolutely everything about it. However, we have notions about abstractions like a city or unemployment, and we call these connected mental images a mental model. In fact, when a senator or president considers what to do about unemployment, he has either some implicit or explicit notions about the probable causes of unemployment and how it will respond to policy changes. It is probably safe to say that most social policy in the United States today is based on implicit mental models held by politicians.

Physical laws are another form of model; often expressed in equation form, physical laws model with paper and pencil what actually happens in some real physical situation. Hence, by using physical laws as models, engineers and physicists can predict how an apple will fall from a tree, how to land a rocket on the moon, or how to split an atom to release nuclear energy.

Computer simulations are yet another type of model. To construct such a computer simulation, analysts take what is known about the operation of a social system, put it in computer code form, and have the computer keep track of the many relationships. Human beings intuit and understand relationships, whereas the computer remembers them and unfolds the consequences of these relationships over time.

We can then tinker with this model of a social process, design, and test new policies. For example, we can build a computer model of an urban area and then institute a housing-revival policy in the simulated reality. We may wish to examine what the impact will be for some particular housing-revival policy, such as massive construction of low-cost housing units. Knowing the response to this policy in the simulated reality, we can in some manner decide whether or not we actually want to institute this policy. Note that instituting a policy on the computer may cost tens or hundreds of dollars. Actually building new housing units could cost millions. Hence, the computer model can help determine the feasibility of new ideas before they are actually implemented.

In summary, a computer simulation, as opposed to other types of models we have discussed, tracks or predicts a complex process over time, monitoring hundreds of interacting variables at any point in time. There are essentially two parts to this process. In the first, the user/analyst specifies relationships believed to be operating in the system and policies that can be used to modify that system. The role of the computer in this particular operation is to accept these relationships within a prespecified format; after the relationships have been specified, the computer then unfolds, rigorously and according to the designed logic, how that system must behave over time. In other words, we specify what we believe are the causes of unemployment, and the computer unfolds what the consequences of the assumptions would be over a five- to ten-year or even fifteen-year period.

It could be argued that the computer is only doing very complicated bookkeeping, which we could do normally ourselves. Consider a student just beginning to study computer simulation. At the end of the student's first term, a typical final assignment might be to build a system model to track fifty interacting variables over a 200-year period. To complete this project, more than 500,000 error-free computations must be carried out by the student. I figured out how many checks I write a year and was surprised to note that I would have to balance my checkbook for a thousand years in order to do the same amount of arithmetic as that involved in the student's final modeling assignment. The speed of modern computing is so great that it allows us to do things that were not, in fact, possible before computers became available. The time needed for the student's project is only several minutes; if charged, the total cost would be one or two dollars.

A FIRST EXAMPLE

A good deal of money is involved in purchasing and producing beef and pork products; the prices of pork or beef or any other commodity are subject to market control. Sometimes there is a good deal of speculation in such commodity markets, so the causes of price fluctuations are worth thinking about. Figure 1 shows some of the relationships believed to be operative in a supply and demand system regulating the price of pork, indicating some of the causal relationships that control commodity prices. Essentially, we are looking at a very simplified causal-loop diagram that shows two basic loops surrounding that variable, the price of pork.

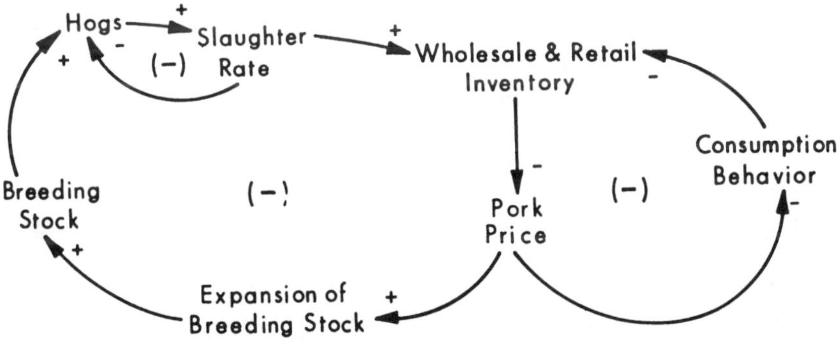

Figure 1. Causal relations involved in pricing pork

Let us look at some of the relationships shown in the figure. If the price of pork increases, consumer behavior will be influenced; if pork becomes more costly, people will tend to buy less of it. Other things being equal, if people buy less pork, over time, pork inventories will increase, and this increase in inventories will drive down the price. Thus, an initial increase in pork prices leads to pressures within the system that eventually decrease the price of pork.

Similarly, if pork increases in price, farmers tend to react by expanding their breeding stocks. Over time, expanded breeding stocks in the Midwest lead to more hogs being slaughtered, which eventually leads to more hogs in butchers' inventory and declining prices. That second loop, the supply loop, also has the effect of stabilizing prices. Quite obviously, both the demand loop and the supply loop tend to drive price into a stable equilibrium. These are the kinds of feedback loops that dominate economic systems, and our example shows a fairly straightforward supply/demand mechanism.

There are only seven or eight relationships in this small model, but how will that model behave over time? One difficulty in determining the price of pork over time results from the lack of precision about each of those relationships. But even if I had been very precise, I doubt that many people could correctly predict how the price of pork behaves over time.

I have already specified what I mean by each of those causal links (e.g., how much will consumption drop off given a 5, 10, or 20 percent increase in the per-pound price of pork) in a computer program. Figure 2 shows the computer's prediction of the price of pork, the price of hogs, and the size of the farmer's breeding stock over a one-hundred-month period. Based on only the causal relationships shown in Figure 1, the model predicts that the price of pork will exhibit regular cyclical fluctuations about every thirty-two months. In fact, real pork prices do show fluctuations similar to those predicted by the model. A more involved version of this model might be used by the USDA to stabilize pork prices on the domestic market.

Most major commodities on a world market, whether pork, beef, jute, or iron ore, exhibit similar cycles. Policies designed to stabilize these cycles are of considerable importance to both producers and those who buy the commodities. An analysis of the system at approximately this level of complexity is capable of shedding light on policies that can stabilize those prices.

Where can we go from here? Having created a model that is capable of replicating problematic behavior, an analyst would now try to devise a policy to stabilize pork prices. For example, can price supports be given to farmers? To retailers? Should the price of feed be supported? There are also a number of policies that might be recommended by the U.S. Congress or the Department of Agriculture to stabilize pork prices. Our simulation would allow us to determine in advance whether or not a particular policy might work. If the model works, we would have greater confidence that a particular policy would also work if it were implemented.

A SECOND EXAMPLE

A more complicated example is a very controversial piece of work completed in the early 1970s. The study considered the depletion of natural resources and the process of development on a global level. This work was first published by Jay Forrester and in a subsequent volume, by a team of researchers at M.I.T. under the general rubric of limits to growth. That study raised the specter of a computer that predicts the

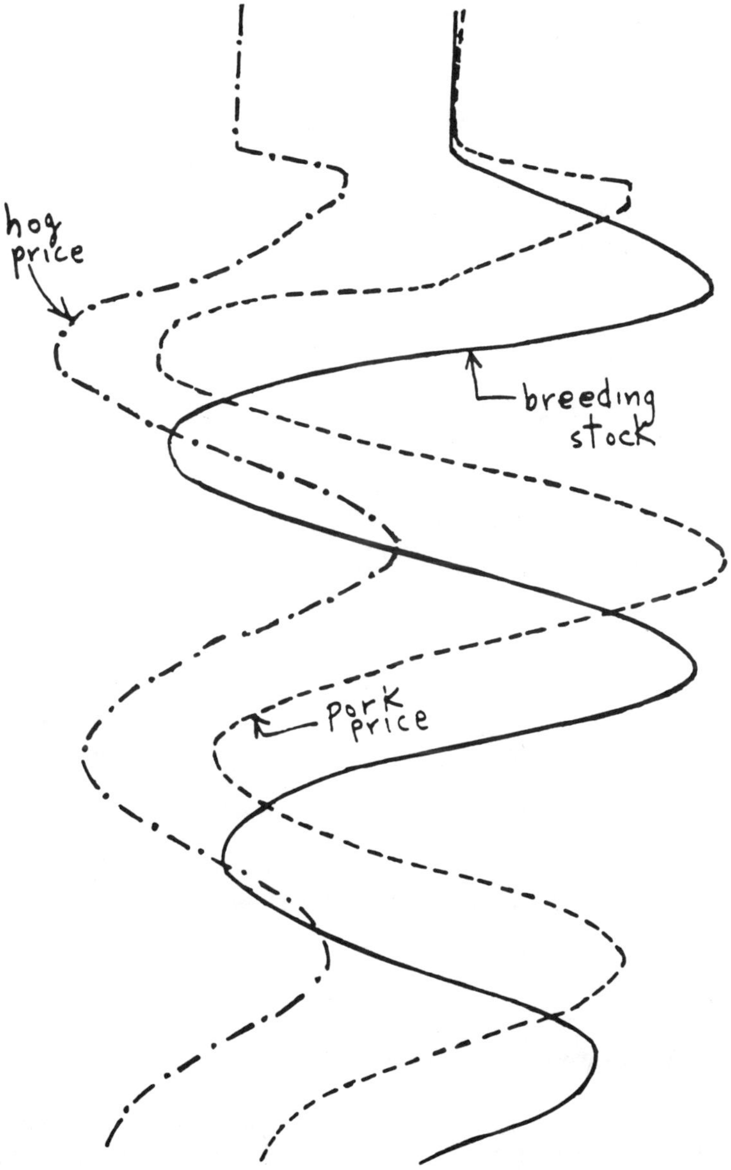

Figure 2. 100-month simulation of breeding stock levels, hog prices, and pork prices based on simple commodity model

future of the world through the year 2100. This particular simulation model began with a series of very plausible relationships between some major interacting variables in a global system and came up with some surprising results.

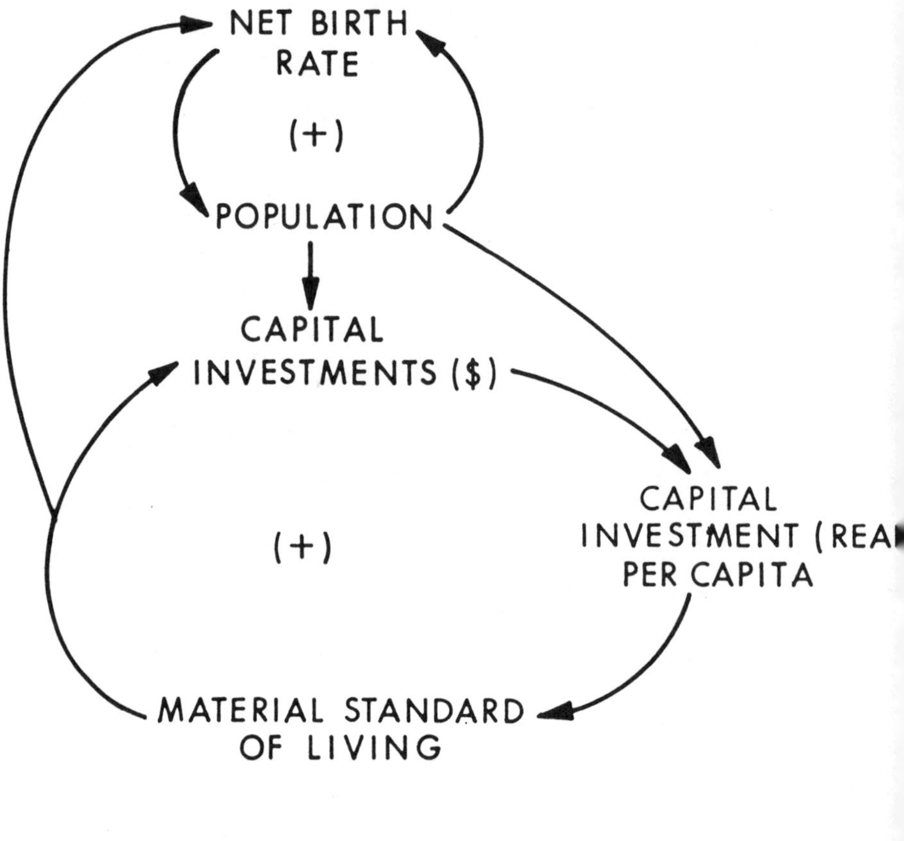

Figure 3. Several causal loops in world-2 model

Figure 3 shows the types of relationships built into the model; they are not difficult to understand. The top loop in Figure 3 shows that if there is a higher net birthrate, there will be increased births and an increase in population over time. If the population is increasing, there are more births (this relationship is based on a proportionality factor). There is a positive reinforcing growth pressure between population and birth. I think those relationships are almost tautological.

Other things being equal, the model postulates that there is a positive relationship between population and capital investment. That is, an increased population generates more dollars to spend on capital investment (using a proportionality factor similar to the one discussed previously). If we divide dollars of capital investment by population, we have capital investment per capita, which is an indicator of such things as how many cars or factories exist per person. There is reason to believe on a very simplistic level that more real capital per person means a higher material standard of living. A series of studies, cited in Forrester's work, note that a higher material standard of living tends to generate more capital investment, which also has a predictable effect on net birthrate.

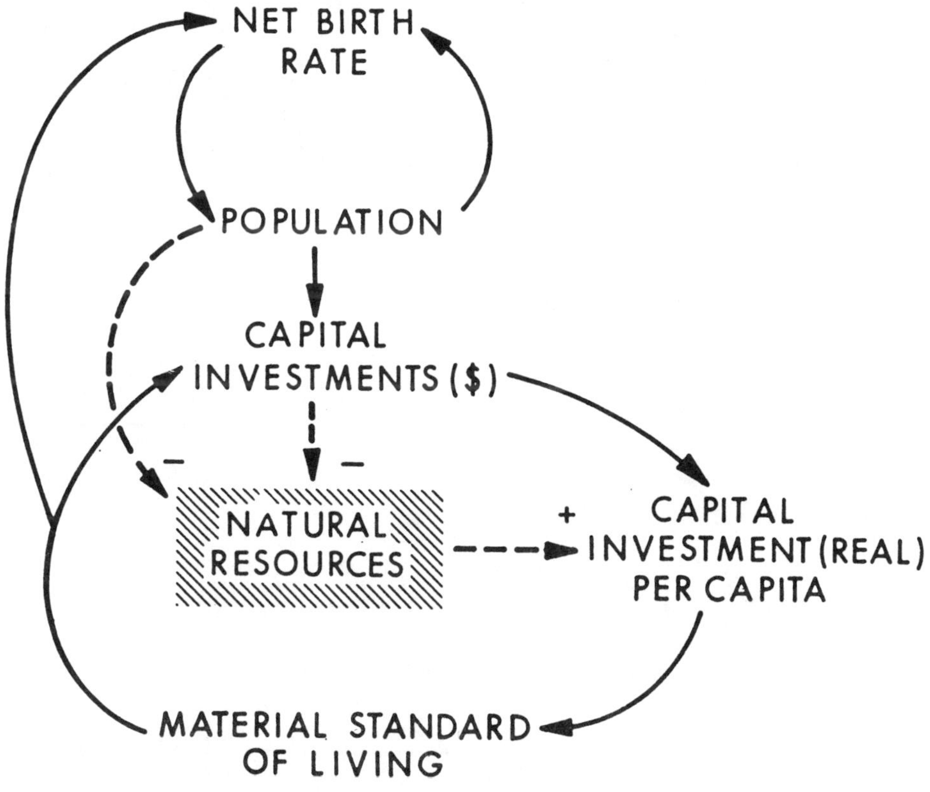

Figure 4. Inclusion of natural resources in world-2 model

Figure 4 builds on Figure 3 and adds slightly to the complexity of the system under study. The dotted lines show relationships that have been added to the original diagram. Figure 4 shows that as population increases and capital investment increases, greater population pressure tends to use up natural resources at a more rapid rate. That is, cars use gasoline, people buy cars, and cars require iron ore. Thus, the more people and capital there are, the faster iron and oil reserves would tend to be depleted.

As natural resources are depleted, it becomes more and more difficult to convert a dollar of capital into real capital; that is, if we have to drill further for oil or if the United States runs out of oil and has to import it, we get less oil per dollar. Similarly, if we have to dig deeper into iron ore mines, we get less iron per $1,000 of capital investment and so on. In sum, the model posits decreasing returns per investment dollar as natural resources decrease in availability. (These are several of the more critical types of assumptions built into this model.)

Of course, relationships in this model enjoy varying degrees of confidence. There are reliable data supporting the relationship between material standard of living and health conditions and birthrate. The

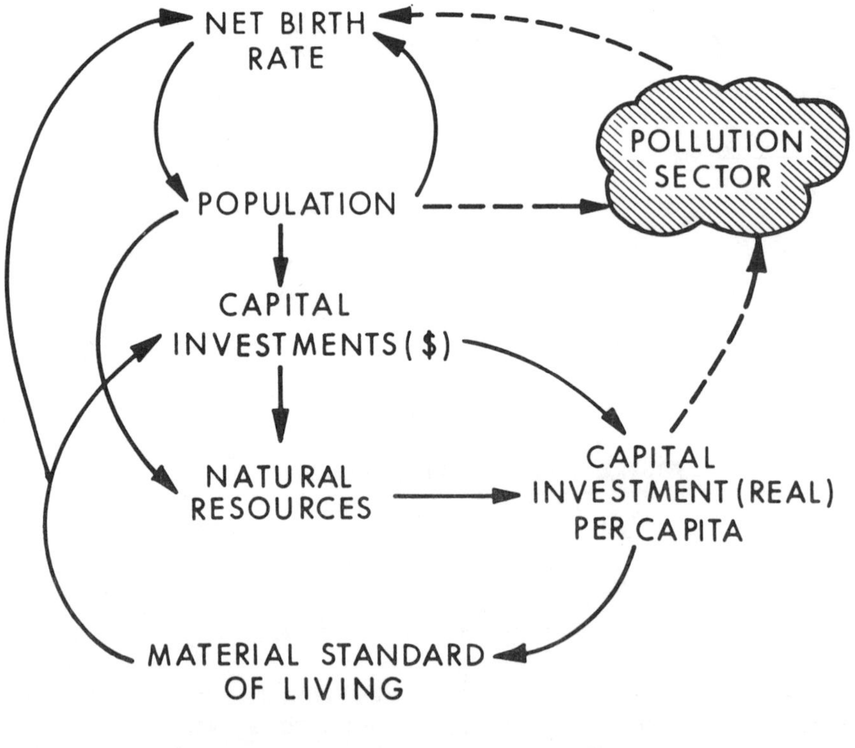

Figure 5. Inclusion of pollution effects in world-2 model

impact of capital availability on the material standard of living is fairly well documented in the economic literature. However, the model goes beyond these well-established relationships and hypothesizes other types of relationships. This is a source of some of the criticism directed at the model, namely, it speculates on certain effects that are not well known—the effect of capital investment, population (fairly well known), and pollution (less well known).

Figure 5 summarizes some of the hypothesized effects in the model due to pollution. These relationships combine some well-established facts with informed speculation. (See question 24 and responses.)

The natural ability of a river to clean itself and the natural ability of the atmosphere to clean itself are included in the pollution sector within the model. The model then hypothesizes that increased population tends to generate more pollutants. The model also speculates on how population and capital investment result in the overall generation of pollution. These postulates are weak, because population and industrial pressures may well combine in some fashion that is simply not understood. The most speculative loop in Figure 5 is the one showing that additional pollution will have a negative impact on the birthrate. There is very little scientific evidence to support that hypothesis, because pollution levels fifty or one hundred times greater than those currently existing have never been experienced worldwide. We have some information from London in the later part of the nineteenth century and early part of the twentieth century about the impact of pollutants in the air on the death rate in London—lung cancer and such things. This evidence was sorted and built into a logical web of reasoning represented by links such as those shown in Figure 5.

Figure 6 is a more technical flow diagram where the causal relationships outlined in previous figures are shown in more detail—one step closer to the form of computer code needed by the machine. The box in the upper left-hand corner represents population; the box in the lower left-hand corner represents natural resources; far over to the right is the box representing pollution. The confusing web of dashed lines indicates assumed causal relationships between various variables, similar to those relationships discussed in previous figures.

Corresponding to each one of those circles, boxes, or valves are lines of computer code, based on an empirical derivation of results for that particular relationship. Each relationship should be substantiated by social scientific research; or in the case of pollution effects just mentioned, based on informed speculation, because there is no empirical evidence of what happens if pollution goes beyond the ranges that historically have been observed. Therefore, the best that can be done under these circumstances is to combine empirical data with informed speculation.

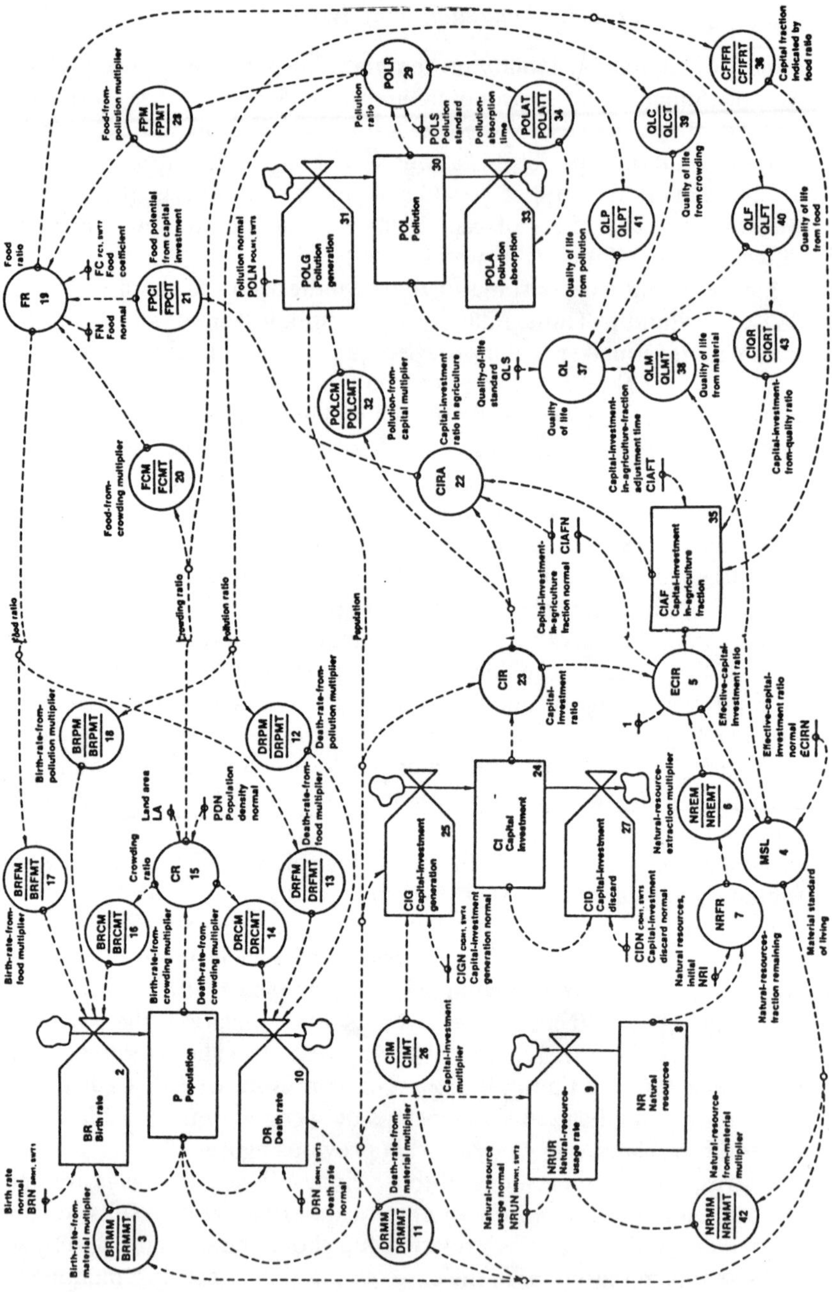

Figure 6. Complete diagram of the world model interrelating the five level variables—population, natural resources, capital investment, capital-investment-in-agriculture fraction, and pollution. (Reprinted from Jay W. Forrester, *World Dynamics*, fig. 2–1, pp. 20–21.)

Such a procedure for hypothesizing relationships certainly leaves one open to criticism if the results are controversial, which, in fact, turns out to be the Achilles' heel of this particular piece of work.

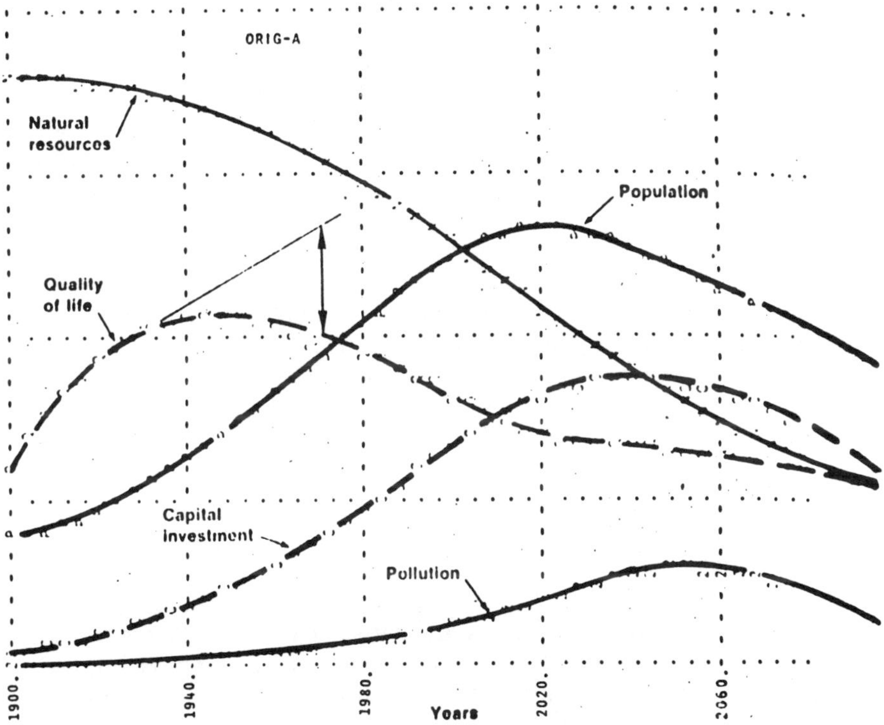

Figure 7. Basic behavior of the world model, showing the mode in which industrialization and population are suppressed by falling natural resources. (Reprinted from Jay W. Forrester, *World Dynamics*, fig. 4–1, p. 70.)

The causal relationships shown in Figure 6 generate a dynamic trajectory indicating what would be the behavior of the system if it were allowed to run free over time. Figure 7 is a projection of the five major variables in that model plotted against time. The horizontal axis is scaled as time from the year 1900 through the year 2100. Population, for example, rises to a peak at about the year 2030 and then declines. The natural resource variable in the upper left-hand corner shows a monotonic decrease through the entire run of the model, with the most rapid rate of decrease being somewhere around the year 2000. The dashed line representing capital investment shows the global level of capital in the world. The lowest dashed line measures the aggregate level of pollution in the world.

This model contains a very controversial twist; the authors included a variable called quality of life, given as an index. Using a prespecified algorithm, the five variables are melded together into a single index, painting a very gloomy picture, indeed. It turns out that somewhere around 1955 things were about the best that they are ever going to be and it is all downhill from there on. This conclusion, of course, is only as true as the assumptions that were built into the model. There is some reason to believe that those assumptions should be subjected to critical scrutiny by a team of analysts other than the authors—in fact, the authors made this statement in their original work.

Figure 8 shows one of a large number of policy tests actually conducted on this model. The initial run of the model (shown in Figure 7) assumes a finite amount of natural resources; however, another team of researchers believes that natural resources are discoverable and not finite. Furthermore, it is possible, through recycling, to slow down the use of natural resources. As an analyst, I can put those assumptions into the model—giving the world twice as many natural resources as initially hypothesized and starting in 1970, allow virtually complete recycling. These changes in assumptions will virtually eliminate the natural resource constraint that caused the decline shown in Figure 7.

If we examined the model carefully, we would see that the declining natural resource curve gradually chokes off capital investment and causes the problems that we saw in Figure 7. This means that in terms of the U.S. economy, the declining availability of steel and oil will eventually interrupt the ability of U.S. industry to continue to capitalize. Thus, it is suggested that we develop infinite sources of energy and completely recycle such usable raw materials as glass and steel and paper and wool.

What impact would this policy have on the model? Notice that in Figure 8, the decline of natural resources is dramatically halted, starting, I believe, in 1975, when this policy is introduced. Consequently, capital investment continues unchecked as compared with the earlier version shown in Figure 7. Capital investment continues to grow at an accelerating rate, and somewhere around the year 2030, the world generates a tremendous level of pollutants, shown by the curve that goes off the top of Figure 8 and comes down later. The model generates a pollution crisis; that is, unchecked industrial development due to increased availability of resources leads to a situation at least as bad as the one we observed in the earlier run. (See questions 21, 22, and responses.) This result may suggest that we should do something else with our infinite amount of technology or infinite amount of resources.

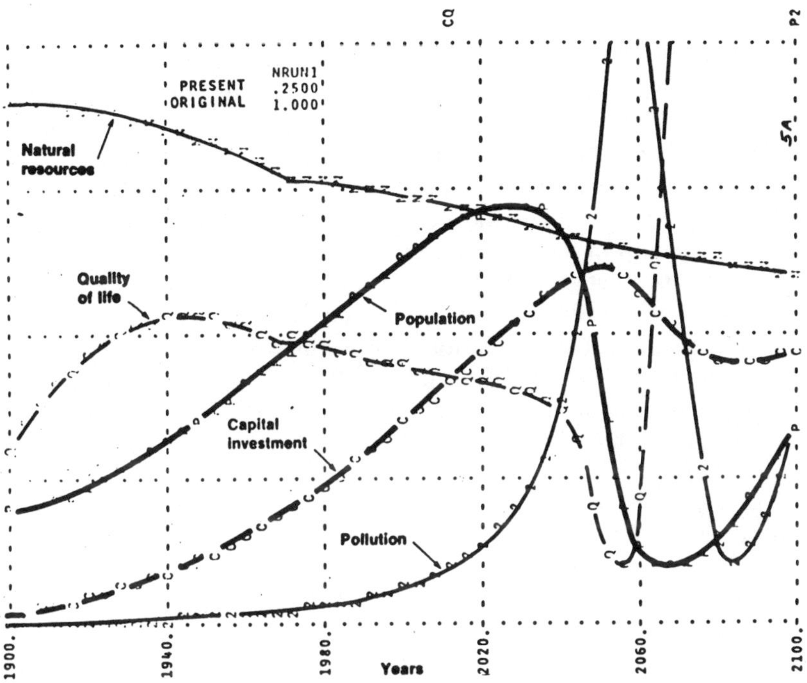

Figure 8. Reduced usage rate of natural resources leads to a pollution crisis. (Reprinted from Jay W. Forrester, *World Dynamics*, fig. 4–5, p. 75.)

Perhaps we should invest more heavily in pollution abatement, and it is, in fact, possible to test such a policy in a laboratory situation.

This example illustrates some of the more dramatic work that has emerged in the field of system dynamics. It is dramatic and controversial research because it deals on a global scale with relationships and time scales that are difficult for people to fully comprehend.

OTHER TYPES OF SYSTEM DYNAMICS STUDIES

Smaller problems, too, are capable of more detailed analysis. A model following essentially the same logic of construction as in the two preceding examples is the basis of much of current U.S. energy policy. To deal with the problem of energy dependence or to understand that complex web of interrelationships, models, such as the model that I have just described, with all of its strong and weak points, are being used as a basis for U.S. energy policy. Consider the impact of instituting a tariff on barrels of oil at some known future time or of increasing a tariff instituted in 1985, for example, through 1995. A simulation would be used to investigate the impact of these policies over time. What happens if a Mideast war occurs at the same time that the tariff occurs? We don't have to speculate about how these policies interact; we can simply run the model again—spend another $1.25—and institute the tariff in conjunction with the Mideast war in 1987 or 1995 or 1999, and the model becomes a powerful heuristic device for showing policy makers what might happen given these circumstances.

A team of researchers at M.I.T. has been working on inflation and unemployment for about seven years, and they are beginning to reach some interesting policy conclusions concerning actions that can be taken by the federal government to combat inflation and unemployment. In fact, the researchers claim that certain actions now being taken by the federal government may be worsening inflation. (See question 15 and responses.)

The Scandinavian governments are interested in how to best preserve natural resources. Analysts can devise wood and pulp-cutting policies and overall harvest policies to optimize the long-run use of Scandinavian forest resources. In addition to models related to social problems, some interesting work has been done in modeling biological systems. Researchers have looked at the generation of insulin in blood sugar and completed some clinical work to improve treatment of diabetics by building a simulation model of the feedback processes involved in diabetic coma and shock. All of these examples are the types of problems to which system dynamics models have been applied. (See questions 16, 17, and responses.)

OTHER TYPES OF COMPUTER-BASED MODELS

Thus far, I have described for the most part a single kind of simulation, system dynamics simulation. But using computers as analytic aids to enhance the ability of human beings to think about social policy problems is not limited to the system dynamics approach. In fact, a wide spectrum of other modeling approaches exists.

For example, econometric models are structurally quite similar to system dynamics models; however, they use data and empirical evidence in a somewhat different way. Random process models are also used to analyze a much narrower class of systems; for example, how to design switchboards in phone circuits and waiting-line processes in production and assembly lines. Optimization models are used to a large degree in industrial-control processes.

These models strive to identify policies that can lead to optimal control of production lines, schedules, and other applications, including the detailed allocation of resources in an optimal fashion. Of course, there is a whole field where people take pieces of models developed in various areas and combine them.

THE DARK SIDE OF "THE FORCE"

I want to dwell for a moment (if I may borrow an image from *Star Wars*) on the dark side of this computing force in the field of social policy analysis. Assume that we are constructing social engineers, people who can design social systems—an elite class of people who know about these models and who can design social policy. These analysts, I have argued, are an asset to society as problem solvers. But turn that same statement around and say that with a slight twinge in your voice. I am not so sure you would always like to have an "elite" core of social engineers designing social policy. Such a notion can be downright chilling.

Analysts in this field are aware of at least three potential dangers; the first one stems from a fundamental paradox. If we have a complex system and devise more and more complex models, our models eventually become so complex that we no longer understand them. This means that some of the models currently being used to simulate social policies are so complex, involving tens of thousands of equations, that the people who construct the models no longer understand why they behave as they do. This is a dangerous situation because at that point the modeler has abdicated control over the policy process. A policy recommendation might then be based on reasoning that would run along the following lines: "I recommend thus and so because I've got this huge model that has 10,000 equations in it, I really can't explain to you what's going on in there, but you really should implement the policy anyway." This is dangerous because simulation results that were not fully understood by anyone might be taken seriously. (See question 14 and responses.)

Even if that situation doesn't occur, there is another dilemma arising from what we might call the cult of expertise. That is, even if I understand what I am talking about and my recommendations are based on complex simulation technology, can a senator or a corporate president understand and have the same confidence in the model that I, as an analyst, have? Why should anyone believe either the model or what I have to say about the model, especially if I am working from a political, philosophical, or ideological base with which decision makers don't agree. Worse yet, my model may subtly incorporate my philosophical or ideological preferences in a way that is not visible to lay decision makers. How can someone argue with me if they don't agree with my conclusions? Are my conclusions due to a difference in ideology or to some technical problem with the model itself? Who can say? (See questions 20, 25, and responses.)

Related to both of these points is the notion of institutional barriers. Some intriguing case studies have emerged showing that in the private sector, corporations are using models as evidence in court. In a recent article, it was noted that Litton Industries had a cost overrun involving the construction of some ships for the U.S. Navy. As these cost overruns were in the billions of dollars, the navy refused to pay the overrun costs, accusing Litton of having been negligent in drawing up their low bid. Litton Industries maintained that change orders sent in by the navy caused the cost overrun. We built a bulkhead, and the navy came in and changed specifications. So we had to carry that bulkhead out and put a new bulkhead back in. It was all those change orders that led to the overruns.

Litton Industries, in order to substantiate their claims asked a modeling team to construct a simulation of the ship-building process with cost equations in order to determine how costly the navy's change orders had been. Consultants came in and built such a model. Analysts then asked the model to build ten destroyers (in simulation) and determine the cost. Then the consultants took that same simulation of the ship-building process and built the same ships except that the simulation was interrupted with a series of change orders such as the ones the navy gave Litton. The model showed that it cost several billion dollars more to build the ships with the change orders.

Litton's lawyers submitted the model and its predictions as evidence that the cost overruns were due to the navy, not to Litton's negligence. It's puzzling to know how a judge then makes sense out of such a claim. To complicate matters even further, the navy then hired another team of modeling experts to evaluate the model, so the judge had to evaluate both the model and the very technical criticism of the model. Is this now a legal question or a technical modeling question?

In areas of social policy design, similar arguments and criticisms are emerging. The same kind of model-based social scientific criticisms has now resulted in a court order that may substantially change the way schooling is financed in the state of New York. How can a judge with legal training interpret technical arguments and decide whether they are correct? The model may not only be incorrect, but there may also be hidden ideological biases on the part of the modelers themselves. In fact, an interesting case study involves the current mandates by U.S. courts requiring busing to achieve racial integration. This mandate is based on a court order that, in turn, is based on fairly complex technical analyses ruled on by the courts. That is, busing was instituted throughout the United States as the result of a number of court litigations based at least in part on a series of results of a fairly involved technical nature. Are our legal and administrative institutions fully prepared to digest and rule on such technically complicated analyses? Currently, in order to ensure independent review and criticism of technical results of social policy design, an expert familiar with both sides of the problem is enlisted to interpret model results.

Any conclusions reached on the basis of technically complex simulation must ultimately be subjected to a clear-thinking test. That is, if the analyst cannot explain in ordinary English how the approach advocated is supported by a particular simulation result, the approach in question should not be followed. Simulations should be used as scaffolding when erecting a building. At the end of the analysis process, we should be able to take away the computer—take down the scaffold—to let the policy decision—the building—stand by itself.

After all these dilemmas have existed for a while, we will gain more experience with the use and misuse of simulations in the social policy context and thereby learn what simulations mean and what they don't mean. As more and more people in the public sector or in business management gain experience with these technologies, we will be in a much better position to use the technologies intelligently. The difficult task is not learning how to use the computer but rather to learn how analysts can grow in their ability to conceptualize and design.

The computer is a powerful extension to the social-policy-design process. Computing in the policy process is positive when it expands the abilities of human analysts by incorporating new dimensions of conceptual and design-oriented thought. On the other hand, we are never free from the potential for misuse. Our challenge is to maximize the new potential for social policy design offered by the computer while dealing effectively with the cognitive and institutional barriers that can lead to misuse of this new technology.

5. *Computers and Communication*

Berton D. Moldow

When computers first began to be used by businesses, in the 1950s, computers and communications were entirely separate entities. Computers were perceived to be "number crunchers"—fast calculators—whose use was justified by reduced labor costs. Early computers were primarily used to perform a priori processes where a well-defined set of instructions performed highly repetitive data processing tasks.

Once cost-justified systems based on well-understood application processes, such as accounting, inventory management, and so forth, were designed, analysts began to seek new uses for computers. For example, before the development of the computer, few industries had been able to effectively use marketing data to forecast sales or to use management optimization tools, such as linear programming. In both cases, mathematical processes were extended beyond the scope of human computational ability.

As application designers developed more complex computer systems, they began to better understand interrelationships between different business processes. Order entry is a good example of a process that had broader ramifications. On one level, the process of order entry required only the creation of an order form. But designers realized that it would also be possible to check the status of inventory and reduce inventory by the order amount. If inventory were below a predetermined value, called an order point, a production order could be generated to replenish stock. The size of a production order also depends on expected sales and the cost of money to carry stock in inventory. There were other relationships as well; for example, order acceptance from a customer could be checked against that customer's credit position. Acceptance of the order could also initiate shipping and billing procedures and lead to a change in accounts payable.

At first, such processes were implemented on computer systems in much the same way that they were performed by different departments, that is, one at a time. Analysts were aware that different departments handled the same data and performed the same processes to produce the same information. As such, computers were not processing information effectively, but with the development of high-speed random-access storage technology, this situation changed. Storage media enabled users to share computer resources, programs, and data and led to the development of computer operating systems and data-base management systems. With these new tools, users were able to manage the sharing of resources more effectively.

The resulting trend toward complex systems required all processing to be performed on a single machine. This requirement demanded more computer power, which meant larger and larger machines. As a result, user computer organizations became more highly centralized, complementing the then widely accepted Grosch's law, which postulated that every dollar spent on a computer would return doubled computer power—in essence, the bigger the better. The acceptance of this rule reinforced growth in the size of computer systems. Analysts assumed that a two-million-dollar computer would provide four times the computer power of a one-million-dollar computer and continued to seek new and more sophisticated application programs to absorb the machine cycles. This in turn led to the growth in size and complexity of computer installations and introduced a new set of problems. Efficient scheduling of machine and personnel resources was chief among them. Managers of production programs, program maintenance, and even new-program development found themselves competing for the use of computer time. The bottlenecks that developed, and the overhead costs that ultimately resulted, reduced the efficiency that centralized installations promised.

The job of getting data to the system and distributing machine-processed material in an accurate and timely fashion also became burdensome. A paper deluge resulted from the batch orientation of processing, the most common mode of operation in the early systems. In addition, few large systems provided immediate access to information. Instead, computer departments had to collect and manually enter data and after processing, burst and distribute reports to locations where they could be efficiently used.

Not to be minimized was a third problem—the creation of a mystique associated with the computing department. Operating departments found themselves dependent on data processing staff, whom they began to regard derisively as the high priests of computing. Department heads wanted to optimize the use of resources necessary for producing the company's product, but in their mind, computer department personnel were more concerned with optimizing the use of data processing equipment. Different objectives, combined with a growing, different terminology, erected barriers that also minimized efficiency. Data processing managers concerned about problems associated with increased centralization sought to overcome these difficulties by bringing computer processing power closer to the ultimate user. They sought to do this by attaching terminals to the centralized processor via communications facilities and by using communications facilities with computers. The marriage of these two technologies—communications and computers—was termed teleprocessing, where *tele* means distant and *processing* refers to processing information. Initially, attempts to merge these two technologies were slow to be implemented, because they required communications equipment that was too expensive. Only a limited number of possible applications justified tying into a processor directly from a terminal.

Consequently, the earliest teleprocessing systems relied on large single applications; the airlines reservation system was an example of an early large dedicated application system. Complementing the emergence of these large systems were specialized communication networks that were dedicated to the specific applications they supported.

Over time, many large multidivisional corporations found they had independently developed and operated several large application-oriented networks. It was common to walk into a sales office and find several different, noncompatible terminals connected via dedicated communications lines to co-located application host-processors. Many of these systems had been implemented with little concern for cross-divisional compatibility. As a result, many expensive networks existed that could not share resources or communicate with each other. Heterogeneity and the resulting incompatibility were, and still are, knotty problems for large corporations.

In the mid-1960s, time-sharing companies and service bureaus, out of necessity, introduced changes to deal with the problems of heterogeneity. Such organizations realized that to market their computer services successfully, they would have to connect different types of terminal devices that potential customers owned with processors that they owned. They also recognized that to attract customers on-line, they would have to find ways of reducing communications costs. Timing was right. The miniprocessor became available at this time, enabling these industries to distribute lower cost processing power to customers via a network that offered significant economic advantage. Before the miniprocessor, customers had to use either a dial line or a leased line to connect a terminal to a remote host-processor application. Since long distance calls were charged according to distance and connect time, customers who sought computer service several times a day for two to three hours or more per day, ran up large telephone bills quickly. If dial-service use were high enough, it would prove more advantageous to lease a circuit at a flat rate; this was still costly and generally resulted in low use.

Service bureaus were able to lower communications costs significantly and permit circuit time-sharing among several users by placing minicomputers between costly communications lines and users. Customers were able to use low local rates to connect terminals to a local miniprocessor that served as a traffic concentrator. The miniprocessor also allowed a single shared circuit to support communications from the miniprocessor to a host processor instead of requiring a dedicated circuit for each terminal. Furthermore, time-sharing companies were able to place circuits between a single miniprocessor and multiple host-processor sites, which enabled users to switch terminals to different sites. This gave users the benefits of the costly dial network at the lower cost of shared leased lines. It also permitted customers to reduce their investment in terminals, since they could use one to access several different application programs. The miniprocessor alleviated interconnection problems between heterogeneous equipment by converting codes and translating protocols.

The use of computers in data communications networks accelerated through the 1970s. If, in the 1980s, the cost of computing continues to decline at a faster rate than the cost of leased or dial communications, this trend will continue, and computers will play an even larger role in data communications than heretofore.

Computer applications have also been increasing in another communication area that is frequently overlooked because it is so obvious—the telephone network. For years, the telephone depended on such mechanical switching mechanisms as rotary stepping switches or reed switches. During the past fifteen years, telephone companies have been replacing their old switching mechanisms with computers. In the process, they have enhanced the plain old telephone service, or POTS, with such computer-provided services as "total telephone." In this service, a computer alerts a speaker to an incoming call, and the speaker can switch from the ongoing conversation to the incoming call and then back again. A computer also enables a user to dial a previously arranged single digit in place of a ten-digit dial sequence and to dial a code to forward all incoming calls to a chosen telephone number.

Because of the application of computer technology, telephone companies and information-processing services will continue to grow closer and overlap during the next few years. For instance, both industries use store-and-forward technology in their service offerings. In the data processing industry, data entered into a terminal is forwarded to a node (generally a minicomputer); information is stored there until a communications line becomes available. Data is then forwarded to a host processor for processing or storage. A terminal can enter information destined for a host processor even while the host processor is being used for some other purpose. A storage device can accumulate data during a prime shift and start the program processing data after that eight-hour prime shift. It is unnecessary for the application program to be on line concurrently with the terminal in order for processing to take place.

The telephone industry's TWX service was the forerunner of this technology. A TWX user generated a message at a terminal and addressed it to some destination; the message could contain data destined for a host processor. In the early days of the service, a message was routed to a central switching point where it was recreated on paper tape. Operators read the address of the message, tore the message off the incoming paper-tape punch, and placed it in a paper-tape reader. The message was then forwarded to the punch closest to its destination. When the destination machine was free, the message was sent. Using computers to switch messages is merely the mechanization of the manual torn-paper-tape process.

What is interesting is that store-and-forward technology is now being applied to voice communications; in Philadelphia, the telephone company is experimenting with store-and-forward speech. If the called party is out, the caller can leave a message in a voice mode, which will be digitized and stored on a file for subsequent retrieval by the recipient much like a telephone-answering service. What is unique about this digitized store-and-forward technology is that the message need not be left in the Philadelphia exchange. For instance, rather than having to use a long distance line between New York and Philadelphia during peak hours, a caller in New York can record a message for a party in Philadelphia on a file in a computer exchange in New York. When communications resources are available, the phone company can forward the message to a file in the Philadelphia exchange. Store-and-forward computer technology thus permits the phone company to schedule and share its communication lines more efficiently and allows the customer to transmit a delayed voice message at a reduced rate.

Experimentation has also been reported on the digitization and transmission of voice signals through store-and-forward data nodes. Conversing parties can interact in real time with no user-perceptible delays even when such nodes are used. Thus, networks designed for carrying interactive data can be used for real-time voice communications.

The increased convergence between communications and computer industries created controversies that the Federal Communication Commission (FCC) decided warranted investigation. In the last fifteen years, the FCC undertook two separate studies to determine if data processing services offered via communications networks should be regulated like other existing communications industry services or should remain nonregulated like computer industry services. The most current FCC ruling states that basic communications service represented by the telephone and leased and circuit-switched services would remain regulated. Such services would be distinguished from value-added services and information services, which would be nonregulated. Competition is likely to increase in nonregulated areas and should result in new and attractively priced services for information consumers.

Some of these new services are already being applied to the informal or hidden infrastructure of business. Early applications of teleprocessing systems dealt with formally structured information-flow patterns. Analysts who designed networks for specific applications were familiar with message sizes, volumes, and points of origin and distribution. Today, with the needs of formal structures being well serviced, users are becoming aware that they need systems to enhance their informally structured communication channels as well. This task is considerably more formidable. How can the forms of communications needed to support informal organizational structures be determined? How can the nature and size of message units required even be decided given that informal organization structures are constantly changing? Much as football coaches change the game plan to fit the strengths of players and the weaknesses of competition, business management changes organizational structure to capitalize on the strength of employees and fluctuations in economic and competitive conditions. Communication channels that support these changes in structure must be equally flexible.

Currently, the mail service and the telephone are the two communication mechanisms most commonly used to support informal communication channels. Each has its advantages and disadvantages: Mail provides a permanent record; telephone conversations are ephemeral. The telephone is considered more readily available and responsive than the mail service; that is, if the caller can succeed in reaching the desired party. There is a game associated with the telephone that has been labeled telephone tag. It occurs whenever it is necessary to reach another person, and the duration of the game is usually proportional to the time zone difference between parties. For example, a caller on the East Coast needs information available from a source on the West Coast. By the time the source arrives at work, the East Coast caller is at a meeting. The East Coast meeting breaks before lunch, and a call is placed to the West Coast. The source just went for coffee but will return shortly. The caller is at lunch when the call is returned. The source of information is in a meeting when the caller tries after lunch, and so forth.

In many offices, people spend much time away from their appointed desks and are difficult to reach. Some experts suggest that the success rate of making contact with the desired information source in a business call is only around thirty-five percent. Telephone tag highlights the need for various alternative, flexible forms of communication. Teleconferencing is one form of flexible communications ideal for supporting the informal organization. It has some of the advantages of both the mail and the telephone system, with few of their disadvantages. Actually, teleconferencing is a generic term that encompasses various techniques of communications between two or more people, which may use audio, video, and/or computer technology.

Proponents of teleconferencing technologies suggest that their use can reduce annual travel budgets in industry and government by 20 percent or more. They also claim that potential savings can go far beyond mere travel expense if employee productivity is taken into account. Some companies have been convinced by these arguments, and with the increasing cost of fuel, hotel accommodations, and restaurant meals, they have begun to install or are planning to install video- and audio-conferencing facilities. But as exciting as such conferencing may appear, I believe there is a newer conferencing technology that, in the long run, will offer greater savings and productivity increase than either audio or video. I refer to computer conferencing, a form of electronic meeting that joins conference participants through terminals using a computer as an intermediary.

In several ways, computer conferencing is an improvement over audio and video conferencing. The first way is what I call synchronization. Both voice and video conferences demand the simultaneous presence of conference participants. While computer conferencing can support conversational modes of communication and can operate synchronously, its ability to store and forward data adds a significant dimension. The use of this method of communication permits large groups of people to confer with one another even when they are separated by geographical distance as well as time. In addition, it is possible for groups of people who are participating in a computer conference to speak or comment at the same time. Respondents can thereby review comments of other participants without waiting weeks for a conference transcript; since we can read faster than we can listen, response time is again made more immediate. Furthermore, such a conference facility tends to reduce the verbosity of the spoken word; we tend to write far more precisely than we speak.

Although few people are trained typists, most can hunt and peck and ultimately acquire adequate skill. Moreover, rapidly growing acceptance of the personal computer will improve key-entry skills in the present and future work force.

Video conference devotees may object that computer conferencing lacks body language, speech inflection, and intensity. They may also point out that graphic information, represented by a still video frame, transmits large quantities of information efficiently (one picture being worth one thousand words). Several recent studies have shown that moving video, which is expensive because of the high capacity use of communications channels, adds little to the effectiveness of a conference. Video attempts to simulate live conferences necessitate building expensive facilities with special camera and audio controls.

At considerably lower expense than video, computers can enhance conferencing through their inherent graphics capabilities. Computer conferencing offers other features that distinguish it from video or live conferencing. Participants can adjust the information-retrieval rate and interrupt reception with little information loss; they can go back in time and review on command. Perhaps most importantly, participants may join a conference any time and from any location, such as their own office, home, or even hotel room. All that is required is a terminal, modem, display, and telephone. The advantages in terms of logistics, convenience, and expense are obvious. (See question 19 and responses.)

I do not intend to imply that the present form of computer conferencing is a panacea; rather, this mode of communications should be regarded as an enhancement of human information exchange. There will always be a need for various forms of communication, and each will prove its worth under specific situations. Computer conferencing is worthy of mention because it is a highly adaptable tool for many various forms of meetings.

To better explain what I mean, let me first describe some services available from Electronic Information Exchange System (EIES), an operational computer-conferencing system developed by Dr. Murray Turoff at the New Jersey Institute of Technology. It offers the following:

A message service that permits messages to be sent to individuals or groups

A conference service that supports exchanges of information on a many-to-many level through sharing a conference file

A notebook service that provides users with work space where they can maintain private information

A bulletin service that enables users to disseminate information about new services or conferences to other system users

A directory that provides background information on the conferees, such as their affiliation, mailing address, telephone number, and interests

A composition service that provides an editor and scratchpads, so that users can compose and edit textual information before entering such information into any of the other categories of service.

An impressive aspect of EIES is its ease of use; it offers many levels of interfacing. The simplest form to use is the menu, where the user is prompted by the system to select the service and features he wants. However, an experienced user soon becomes familiar with the services and can directly cue the system with the appropriate numerical menu entries. This reduces the number of exchanges that take place between user and system. The user can turn off the menu display by command, which is the next level of user interface. One feature of the command interface is the consistency of semantics, which permits the user to almost guess at a command. Another appreciated feature is the forgiving nature of the system in the case of an incorrect entry. For example, menu mode requires the display of three screens of information before the users can compose a message. In command mode, a single entry +CNM (+ signifies the beginning of a command statement, and CNM stands for compose new message) brings the user to the same point. It is impossible to describe the simplicity of the EIES command interface; it must be experienced.

Electronic Information Exchange System also offers a development language called INTERACT. The EIES designers recognized that participants may wish to confer in different formats or via customized interfaces; they may wish to follow *Robert's Rules*, allow inquiries and responses to questions, or ignore form totally. INTERACT permits conferees to design any structure they feel is appropriate and to define their own special command interface. INTERACT users, however, must be more experienced than the casual participant. The EIES system does provide consultants who may be queried about new structures or hired by a conference group to program new features into the INTERACT language.

The EIES conference on hepatitis is an example of a private computer conference. This conference, sponsored by the National Institute of Health, set out to accumulate an authoritative and usable set of knowledge on the subject of hepatitis. Over an extended period of time, several experts on hepatitis, who would have been unable to meet because of demanding schedules and geographic separation, participated in a conference on the EIES system. With EIES, all participants were able to remain in their own work environments; have access to their notes and reference material; and still share information, thoughts, and ideas with others. Over a period of a year and a half, this group of experts digested several thousand documents, reviewed and commented on contributions by their peers, and developed a single authoritative source of 1,500 pages. This information is cataloged in the NIH Medlark data base and is now an available reference source.

Two excellent examples of tailored structures on EIES are Politech and Tours. Politech, a question-and-response type of structure, and its derivative Legitech, were initially designed for state legislatures. Twenty-five state legislatures in the United States and six federal government agencies now participate in this conference, which addresses common legislative problems about such issues as pollution, mass transit, and waste disposal. In effect, any state legislature or government professional among the participating groups has access to a host of experts who may have already dealt with a similar problem in their own locale. Not only does Legitech save valuable time, but it is contributing to improved decision making from state to state.

Tours, a structure that can be effectively used as an educational tool, permits a moderator or authorized participant to write scenarios and organize them into tree structures. Other participants, such as students, read and comment on these individual scenarios. The scenarios can be a set of historical statements, a description of an algorithm on how to solve a mathematical problem, and so forth.

User surveys and experiments on EIES performed by Roxanne Hiltz, with a grant from NSF, revealed some notable user characteristics. Users claim that the conferencing format forced them to judge participants by their entry-information content rather than sex, height, or appearance. They remarked that without distractions from a communicator's presentation skills, they were more aware of the information exchanged.

Experiments also showed that users were more likely to contribute in a computer-conferencing environment than at a face-to-face conference; women especially participate more freely, no longer subordinates who defer to their managers in face-to-face conferences. The system sometimes encourages participation by offering the users anonymity; in fact, users may optionally sign a pen name instead of their own name.

A good example of the use of anonymity on EIES was an application used for standards development. Typically, competing companies must cooperate to develop standards for their industry's products. Yet committee participants are understandably reluctant to discuss the implications of new technology lest they disclose proprietary information. Computer-standards conferences with anonymity enabled participants to offer suggestions and ideas more freely than when they could be identified.

Teleconferencing may be one of the more exciting uses of computers in communications, but it is by no means the only new entry. Electronic mail, office automation, and video-tex also merit mention. Electronic mail delivers messages to a person's electronic mailbox instead of a physical mail box. Several commercial systems are already being offered to business by the Tymnnet and Telenet value-added networks. AT&T will publicly provide similar message services through its Advanced Communications Service (ACS).

The implications of office automation extend well beyond word processing, which is primarily a secretarial tool. Before long, office automation equipment will enhance the capabilities of principals, namely, the managers and professionals within an office. Office automation will provide access to data bases of information, offer messaging and conferencing facilities, provide for electronic calendars and filing, and so forth. It is a development that will be aimed at enhancing the production of the white-collar worker. If we consider that 75 percent of the expense of running an office is the salaries of managers and principals, with salaries one of the fastest rising costs in industry, the significance of this type of development is easy to grasp.

Video-tex, a development pioneered in the United Kingdom, provides information to the home television or personal computer by telephone lines or CATV links. Data bases already exist from such companies as CompuServe, The Source, and Dow-Jones. This service is now offered commercially in England under the name PRESTEL, and there are more than forty experiments around the world that are attempting to introduce new services to businesses and the home. For example, in Coral Gables, Florida, Knight-Ridder, with AT&T, is offering in-home banking, teleshopping, and theater and air line ticket purchases. The best known experiment in this country is Qube, offered by Warner-Amex in Columbus, Ohio. Other experiments are currently under way in Japan, Canada, Europe, and the United States. In France, PTT proposes to give a terminal to home subscribers at cost ($100) or even free because of the savings on the cost of printing and distributing telephone books.

There can be little doubt that the marriage of computer and communications will affect social, political, business, and economic patterns significantly in the next decades. It is difficult to predict how vast these changes will be. (See question 18 and responses.) Consider the development of the printing press in the fifteenth century; within thirty years of its invention, there was a press in every major city in Europe. The widespread printing of bibles created a demand for education and literacy that altered the church's role as keeper of knowledge. No one could have foreseen the fundamental changes wrought by this invention. The merger of computer and communications technology will prove at least as revolutionary a development, and we should expect significant change.

Marshall McLuhan commented that people customarily go through life looking out of a rear-view mirror. Like the other contributors to this volume, I have tried to provide a perspective afforded by peering through the windshield. The problem is that although we are looking forward we can only see to the peak of the hill or the bend in the curve up ahead. Some can look beyond and see the rise of the hills or the curves in the road beyond. But they are not capable of saying if distant points will be reached or how far they are. That is the position we find ourselves in today. We can catch glimpses of what might be from the technology, but can only guess what the future holds.

6. *Questions and Replies*

David F. Andersen and Berton D. Moldow

Question 14: Mr. Andersen, I have three interrelated questions. First, how accurately can predictive systems, such as the econometric and other social-science based models, predict events? How does the model's predictive ability compare with the predictive ability of an informed, intelligent expert on the same kinds of things? Second, isn't it always possible for such a system to come up with an excuse? For example, if the model fails to predict what it claimed it could, the reason given for failure may be that either enough variables or the right variables have not been considered. And finally, if a system is used to determine what will result from a particular response, can such a system at least recommend a solution? Presumably, a human being will make the decision to implement a policy, not the machine, although a machine indicated the solution. How can a human being agree to a machine-indicated solution?

Andersen: I don't think a machine can either predict the future or make decisions. I think judgments about the future are certainly in the political and the corporate arena, and they are made by political decision makers and chief corporate officers. I have never seen a situation—except in production-operations and engineering systems—where predicted output from a machine was used to make a major policy decision. If you expect a model to "point" predict the future, I am very pessimistic about that happening, and since I don't believe that can be done, I think it would be a very bad idea to try to use decisions based on such point predictions. We are trying to enhance our intuition and our understanding of a system. I return to the scaffolding analogy I used before. First we design a model for some particular policy problem and examine an associated series of solutions. Then we remove the computer from the picture and ask ourselves if the predictions and solutions make sense intuitively. And if the results that have been predicted or the decisions that have been advocated by a computer cannot stand up to scrutiny by an assembly of informed decision makers, then I would say don't pay attention to them. I have not seen situations where people in key decision-making roles have used point predictions or relied on them. The machine should not be used blindly to make decisions or point predict; it is like any other enhancing tool—it helps us understand how a system behaves.

Question 15: Is there quite a bit of evidence to show that by using this kind of simulation, the quality of decisions does, in fact, improve?

Andersen: I have to speak from my own personal experience in specific cases where we have been involved. Around 1973, we were able to predict shortfalls in U.S. enlisted-manpower projections due to a computer simulation that only took into account the consequences of an all-enlisted force; this was something that had not been anticipated by previously existing analysis. In a project for the state of Massachusetts on projecting the cost of education programs, a computer-simulation run resulted in a far better estimate than simulations based on expert judgment. Therefore, individual cases existed where we obtained a much better view of the future. The notion that a computer can predict the future any better than the data that is used or can make decisions is very dangerous; if I left that impression, I did not intend to. Still, I can point to examples from my own experience where a simulation model has enhanced administrative decision making to the extent of saving hundreds of millions of dollars in public funds.

Moldow: Often simply going through the development of a model is valuable even if the model is never actually run, since it provides better understanding of the decision processes. Secondly, when you do have a model, you can use it for determining sensitivity. Sensitivity analysis indicates how changing a specific parameter affects outputs. Certain parameters can vary widely and have little effect on the output. We don't have to track those parameters, because they are of no great concern; that is useful information. Unfortunately, there is no criterion that shows whether or not a variable of importance was missed.

Andersen: To develop a corporate model, for example, an analyst would interview people throughout the corporation to find out what was going on in sales, production, accounting, and inventory management. Similarly, a task force might be put together to study state finances. Now just the process of assembling those people in a very structured environment helps show what is going on in that corporation or that financial system. The process of bringing together ten experts to discuss the structure of that system would be a useful exercise even if we never went to computer code. To a large degree, I believe that the interaction process and the model-building process are as valuable as the formal published report.

Question 16: Performance tracking seems to be one of the important features of model building and planning. When we are examining a complex future in the public policy area, trying to make decisions, are models used to do a better job of selecting the right data and then tracked over a period of time to see how the model is, in fact, performing? Can current data then be compared with what was predicted earlier and used to evaluate the model?

Andersen: For most models, one of the criteria is how well a model can predict the past. We are very good at that. We can very accurately predict what happened between 1960 and 1980 and explain it. Of course, a problem arises when we turn to 1990, because we don't have data for 1980–1990, so we don't know whether the predicted relationships will hold. There is no tried and sure way, for example, of knowing whether a factor that has not been anticipated will come into play. All the testing in the world will not help, since the only data available are historic. But this situation is no different from that in any other policy-making or decision-making process. Somehow, odd things do occur, and simply because we use a computer model does not mean that the model will somehow be more scientific or more exact than it would be without machine assistance.

Question 17: These models remain in use for some time. Consequently, if in 1977, you analyze a problem and extrapolate to 1990, will three new years of data in 1980 indicate the accuracy of the 1990 prediction?

Andersen: There has been some follow-up study on econometric models that has looked at prediction results, and they have had very poor performance records recently. Other models have had quite good performance records. Some corporate simulations have shown anticipated future downturns in profits, which have, in fact, occurred. I worked on a team that did a simulation of educational finance, and the simulation predicted the repeal of a law, which has actually occurred. Regarding the idea of shortfalls in manpower in U. S. enlisted people, a study I did in 1974, I believe, predicted the 1980–1981 issues that took place in that election. There are some existing published models from the mid-1960's that predicted a dramatic rise in gasoline prices due to shortages.

Question 18: What does your crystal ball reveal about home-computer network activity? Does the communications industry have the capacity to support this trend without experiencing channel saturation?

Moldow: I predict that by 1985, ten percent of the homes in the United States will have access to computer service by telecommunications facilities of some sort. Capacity is really no problem, surprisingly enough; by 1985, better than sixty percent of the homes in the United States will have access by CATV to wide-band communication services that are bidirectional. If CATV links are not sufficient, the FCC is currently licensing low-power television in local regional areas, and those stations are being picked up. When we consider interactive communications and video-tex, we recognize that the volume of output information coming from the computer to the home display or the home video screen, relative to the volume of information then transmitted by the user requesting information, is going to be in the magnitude of perhaps one thousand to one. Given this ratio, it is conceivable that we will be able to use a conventional telephone line or perhaps a packet-switching service, which would be even less expensive, to make a request to the computer and receive information by broadcast facility. There are other alternatives. Obviously, we are going to see increases in capacity, for example, with fiberoptics. If we consider the ratio of output to input, we see that capacity is not going to be a problem.

Question 19: Based on your comments about information and communication and some of the networking that you have, it seems that traditional education will soon become antiquated. Would you comment on what sort of role this communication ability and information access will have in education in the future?

Moldow: I think there is going to be a marriage of technologies in support of education and not only in the video-tex environments. There is already some very interesting work going on today using video-disk technology in education—in particular, the Phillips technology, with the laser. It provides search- and freeze-frame capability. Certainly, we can put textual information on a video disk; we can also supplement textual information on the video disk with lecture material. With the video disk, an instructor can program sequences of events for a student, or the student can program his own sequence, based on his background and his capabilities. Now join that technology, first a reading level and a quiz level supplemented by the author's visual presentation supplementing the information, perhaps enhancing it with examples offered by computer conferencing. If, after having read and seen the material, students have questions, they can anonymously, or by using their name, request the instructor to answer questions. In essence, what will be provided is a one-to-one, student-to-instructor ratio.

Andersen: I have to add a somewhat dissenting note. My experience has been that students and teachers seem to resist innovations to a large degree and perhaps rightly so. In our pilot testing in secondary schools, we have seen that although new methods and computer-enhanced curricula are available, algebra is really algebra and history is history, and people who teach algebra and history don't feel the need for this technology. It takes a long time for me in my own teaching to change my methods, and I think that is going to be the greatest drawback in curricular innovation.

Question 20: I haven't seen a great deal of research on changes in social relationships between people that is associated with the introduction of this technology. Given the massive influx of new technology, it seems that there will be dramatic social changes reflected in the size of educational institutions and offices if these new technologies are adopted. What are the implications if we are concerned with interactions that involve not merely transmitting knowledge, but with information on how to behave, on imagination, manners, what is right, power relationships, and so forth. These subjects form a hidden curriculum that will be neglected by the machine. Has there been any research on these topics?

Andersen: I am not directly familiar with research on that topic. I am familiar with the effects of introducing technology into public and private organizations. For example, when portfolio management is introduced in banks where formerly there had been a portfolio and a manager who made investment decisions, but now his investment file drawer is replaced by a computer terminal which has access to tremendous analytic capabilities, what does that do to the portfolio manager and his job in terms of his feelings that his expertise is being circumscribed by relying on computer judgment? Our school has done a nationwide study of a similar problem on the impact of job-matching systems. It used to be that a professional would counsel people in a very serious way, but if that professional now interacts with the applicant via a terminal, what does that do for that person's perception of himself in his job role? Professional and clerical roles are dramatically redefined under those circumstances, and a large body of literature discusses why things don't work due to lowered self-image in the job role.

Question 21: One of the fundamental characteristics of a model in engineering is that we are eventually able to design an experiment, which, if it succeeds, shows that the model is wrong. I am not familiar with anything equivalent to this in social modeling. Instead, if the model doesn't have the predictive value that was expected, another variable is added or some of the original variables are modified or both.

Andersen: There are a large number of tests that demonstrate model failure; they vary from field to field. There are commonly accepted standards of validity in the field of econometrics. Standard statistical techniques are being refined all the time in terms of a model's ability to fit and predict historic time series.

Question 22: But that is curve fitting.

Andersen: There are a large number of exercises to which a model is subjected, any one of which is capable of casting doubt on a model. These exercises examine both the output trajectory of the model and its causal assumptions. For example, if we had a system that was stable under normal operating conditions but when pushed to a logical extreme point exploded, it is generally accepted that the model exhibiting this type of instability would be discounted.

Question 23: Weren't there instabilities in the results presented in the Club of Rome report, for example?

Andersen: In this particular case, the model is, in fact, asymptotically stable. There is a very rapid overshoot, shown in Figure 8 (p. 101). If the plot were rescaled, we would see that the model doesn't become unstable. The function is not discontinuous at any point in time. However, there are assumptions built into the model that I, personally, have come to question seriously, so I would agree that there are implausible formulations in terms of the ability of an ecosystem to absorb pollutants. But that question is quite apart from whether or not the model passed a stability test. There are other tests that could be applied to this particular model that would cast some serious doubt on the model's structure, and I think the author of the model would also agree.

7. *Computers, Armaments, and Stability*

EUGENE B. SKOLNIKOFF

The focus of this chapter on computers, armaments, and stability is the role of computers in military strategic affairs and the degree to which computers add to or reduce the problems of change, particularly sudden change, in international affairs. It is not a subject that has received much careful analytical attention, and it raises many issues well beyond computers themselves.

Stability is a term that has been used a great deal in the last few decades in analyzing and discussing strategic relationships. Unfortunately, it is a term that is still poorly defined. It is one of those words for which everyone has some sense of the meaning, but is rarely used in any precise analytical sense. I will use it to indicate general concern for the degree to which the international system is resistant to sudden change. How does computer technology make the international system more or less unstable, or more or less vulnerable to disruptive change?

A discussion of the interaction between strategic affairs and computer technology requires several critical observations. It is obvious that the effects of computers cannot be precisely predicted if for no other reason than because the technology is very dependent on research and development. In fact, frontier research and development, and even scientific developments that will affect computer capabilities, are impossible to know with any certainly or precision. The possible developments in artificial intelligence discussed above, for example, demonstrate well that just what form, and in what manner a field will develop and what the particular applications will be is inevitably uncertain. We can have a general sense of it, but it is not possible to preclude surprise.

Moreover, the significance of computer developments usually occur, not in computers alone, but in combination with other kinds of technological or social developments, so that the real significance depends very much on what happens in other fields as well. For example, much of the impact of computers in information processing and handling, has been in conjunction with developments in communication. It is the combination that has made an enormous difference. Similarly, computers would be much less useful in military weapons systems today if it were not for concurrent developments in miniaturization and small-scale electronics. And the role of computers in weapons depends very much on developments in fire power and the destructiveness of weapons systems. It is the combinations that produce the major effects.

Of course, it is insufficient and quite misleading to speak of military armaments as the only determinant of security. National security has always depended—and is likely to become increasingly dependent—on much more than force structures and force capabilities. Many other parts of an economy or of a society and other areas that we normally think of in non-military terms are relevant to security in quite direct ways. Computers have an important role in this broader context to which I will return later.

In addition, the effect of computers may be as significant or as critical in psychological and political areas as they are in actual technological functions. In fact, this aspect of stability is likely to have even greater importance in the future. Because we cannot know the effects in detail, the predictions are likely to be ambiguous. In fact, a word of warning. A number of my comments are likely to be rather negative about the role of computers. It is not so much questioning their importance, or their necessity, or the fact that they are going to be developed and used in multitudinous ways. What I want to do is single out some of the dangers and concerns that need attention and point out some of the negative effects without really challenging their importance or their necessity. In that sense, computers are like most technologies; that is, they can be used for good or ill or are capable of "dual use" for civilian or military purposes equally. An understanding of the dangers, however, is necessary for designing measures to prevent or eliminate those dangers.

Let us first consider some of the applications of computers in weapons systems, most of which will be familiar. In strategic, offensive weapons systems—that is, in intercontinental missiles, submarine-launched missiles, air-launched missiles, cruise missiles, and short- and long-range aircraft—computers have become an essential component. This includes their role in the initial development of the weapons; in target selection; in the ability to hold the weapons on alert, to fire them rapidly, and to control the actual firing process; in the navigation and control of the weapons once launched; and for multiple-warhead missiles, in the separation of the warhead into some number of smaller warheads that are guided to independent targets. All of those processes depend on computers and the ability to build computers into the systems themselves. We must also recognize that not only the design and operation of weapons systems require computers, but the maintenance, repair, and testing as well.

Cruise missiles are an interesting example of an old weapons system transformed by computers. Cruise missiles are essentially unmanned airplanes, developed to great sophistication primarily in their ability to travel at low altitude over unknown or foreign terrain and hit a target with great accuracy. This capability requires computers in design, navigation, and control of the actual cruise to the target. Curiously, I used to work in the Pentagon many years ago when drone airplanes were the new weapons system. This was in the late 1950s when they received much attention and interest. However, ballistic missiles were coming along at the same time. Of course, the Services thought that aircraft were somehow old hat. There was no glamour attached to them, and hence little money; the glamour and the money went to ballistic missiles—not to these airborne, airbreathing missiles. The result was that essentially all of the airbreathing missile developments were stopped in the late fifties in favor of ballistic missiles. Now, of course, the wheel has turned again and glamour has returned to the airbreathing missiles which are similar in concept to what we had in the late fifty's. Now they have more sophisticated controls and navigation, but basically are the same kinds of systems. One can't help but ask how the weapons and the other armaments might have developed and what differences there would be from existing systems had we followed through on these systems that were thrown out because they weren't glamourous enough to attract the interest of the Services or Congress.

In the defensive area, there is an enormous dependence of all the air and ballistic defense systems on computers. These systems require the reduction of large amounts of data into useful information that can be used to evaluate the threat, meet it if required, take whatever defensive (or offensive) action is warranted, or even trigger a massive nuclear response. And, this data processing requires high speed, real-time analysis that stretches the capacity of computers, even the large-scale computers we have today. Antisubmarine warfare (ASW) capability also requires enormous data-handling capabilities. Currently, our strength in this area is based on the ability to collect and process data being received from a multitude of sensors in the oceans. Antisubmarine warfare capability is, in fact, quite primitive. While the sensors may be very sophisticated, the system uses a brute-force approach in which submarines are found and tracked mainly by dint of having massive amounts of equipment in place. It is conceivable that in the future, the ability to track submarines may change through presently unavailable technological development. I am conservative on the time frame, but I suppose that some day it will be possible to track submarines from a satellite or other remote sensor by the ability to look through the ocean. At the moment, we do not have that, and ASW is simply achieved by having listening posts in many, many places. For now, data are transmitted to a central point for analysis. Obviously, a critical feature of that analysis is the ability to handle large amounts of data and to reduce the data to something meaningful.

In conventional warfare, the dependence on computers is also great and growing rapidly. It may be, in fact, that this area of weapons development will undergo the greatest change in the near future. Both fighter and attack aircraft are designed to operate at very high speeds. Pilots in such planes cannot depend on visual means for acquiring targets or detecting and tracking opposition aircraft. They depend on computers for target acquisition, for fire control, for operation of the plane itself, for navigation and coordination with other planes, and for ground control reconnaissance. In fact, American aircraft tends to be much more sophisticated in its use of electronics and computers than Soviet aircraft. Our assumption is that we are compensating for fewer numbers with higher capability. That is an important and often controversial assumption.

Currently—and in the future to an even greater extent—ground weapons will also depend on computers for their operation. For targeting and reconnaissance, antitank and antipersonnel weapons can no longer be used by ground troops on their own, limited by line of sight or visibility; their weapons require processing and control. The same comments apply to naval weapons at sea. Space weapons, too (for example, killer satellites), depend on computers for firing, tracking, acquisition, navigation, and positioning.

In general, conventional warfare weapons are becoming increasingly complex and as a result, difficult to maintain, service, and control. Looking ahead, developments in computers combined with miniaturization and greater reliability may undergo the same type of development as have hand-held calculators. That is, we may move from systems that we now consider complex, obsolete, and difficult to maintain (for example, the old mechanical calculator), to those that are reliable, easy to use, durable, and inexpensive (which presumably characterize electronic calculators). However, while we may assume that the objective of current development is to create systems whose dependence on computers also reduces their vulnerability and complexity, the history of weapons-systems development does not bear that out. Our dependence on computers in weapons systems is too often a vulnerability when it should be the opposite.

Two other aspects of security are intelligence and early warning, each of which requires systems to collect large amounts of data, and process that data rapidly or in real time. In fact, one of the objectives behind the development of the largest computer systems is the need of national intelligence. The National Security Agency is a major user of large-scale computers and in that role, acts as a major driving force for the whole industry. In the case of early warning, information from elaborate radar and surveillance systems must be processed in real time, requiring the use of very large-scale computers. The early-warning use of computers raises some crucial questions, such as how reliable these computers are, how precise is the interpretation of data, and what is the danger of an error initiating a military response. The question as to whether we should ever have a "strike on warning" system—that is, whether we should have a system in which we respond to a computer indication that an attack is underway—is a disturbing and current one.

A major area of military responsibility, heavily dependent on computers, is called command, control, and communications. We rely on that capability to maintain human control over highly destructive weapons as well as to be able to respond effectively to whatever challenge we face. For the intercontinental systems, where the time of delivery is under thirty minutes, the need for extremely rapid information processing, handling, and interpretation of what is or is not coming (in case of a false warning) is critical. Decisions have to be made rapidly. Is a human being quick enough to decide? Is a computer system capable enough to decide? This either-or proposition is critical for a number of systems. The more complex weapon systems are, the more difficult is actual control of the system. In time of warfare, to what extent can we rely on preprogrammed responses?

In addition to problems of control in a time of crisis, computers are necessary for testing and maintaining these systems. Of course, we hope that neither the strategic systems nor the local conventional systems, for use in so called local war, will ever have to be used. Yet we and potential adversaries have to know if they will work or at least have reason to believe they will. The principle of deterrence implies that we have a system that can and will be used if necessary. It is essential that our nation be able to demonstrate that the system can be used. This requirement implies that the system has to be tested, but for nuclear and strategic systems, testing must be in a nondestructive, nonhostile environment. Computers are required as a major part of that testing procedure.

In nearly every phase of these systems problems we also have to be concerned with security of communications. Consequently, cryptography has become an increasingly esoteric art that has moved to the frontier of mathematical research. We have been treated to the spectacle, yet unresolved, of basic research in the highest realms of theoretical mathematics, being classified by the government and removed from the public domain. The particular actions have been rescinded but the problem remains.

There is another critical factor of a different kind: the R&D process itself. The current estimate is that in weapons development, the United States has roughly a five- to ten-year lead over the Soviet Union in most if not all electronic and computer related areas. Research and development is clearly a major factor in maintaining that lead. It affects all of the things already mentioned: weapons design, control and communications, maintenance and testing, software development and the continued developments in cryptography and the security of systems.

The last topic in the direct military area involves the general subject of planning. In the security area, strategic relationships require planning of a kind not relevant in the past; we now find computers being used extensively in the same ways described by Mr. Andersen. In particular, very elaborate models are used to structure and examine strategic relationships. One aspect of these models is the use of computers to simulate war games, attempting to predict in advance complex relationships in time of crisis or attack. In addition, computers are used in the traditional functions of logistics, spare parts, pay, transport, manpower recruitment, and budgeting.

It would be misleading to think of security in only its traditional military dimensions. It is necessary that we consider some global relationships that are not usually thought of in strategic terms. For example, consider the areas of weather and climate. As we learn more about what drives the global weather system and how it changes over time, we will eventually be able to control that weather system. Research on global weather is progressing rapidly, but it depends peculiarly on massive computer capabilities for real progress. The improved knowledge of weather and climate, particularly greater ability to predict and perhaps influence them, will have large positive value for society. But that enhanced knowledge, over time, will also create a new capability for use of weather in strategic terms. That's not something necessarily to look forward to, but we have to be realistic about the fact that knowledge does, always, have this dual application.

More generally, any form of "resource" warfare depends on a knowledge of the global or national resource situation. Mineral resources, water resources, and crops become an important part of the strategic equation, particularly if those elements are likely to change or can be altered. Even monitoring what is happening may be important in certain situations. For example, over a period, it may be quite useful to know what the state of the Soviet Union's crops is, especially if they may be vulnerable to, or have been affected by, disease or adverse weather conditions. The Landsat satellite does give us the capability of monitoring crops, water availability, and items of that kind over the whole globe. That information, together with knowledge of resource dependencies and detailed knowledge of a country's internal situation, can have an important use in foreign policy terms. A country may, for example, be susceptible to foreign-policy pressure or foreign-policy initiative based on knowledge of particular resource strains. It is conceivable that over a number of years longer range strategic factors could be influenced from outside. All systems that provide resource-related information on a national or global scale require computers to function.

Incidentally, the Landsat system is undergoing substantial improvement—improvement that creates both benefits and risks. The resolution of the cameras that are to be used in these resource satellites in the future is going to be much greater than present models. We will be able to see in the public domain information now available only from classified intelligence satellites. The information will be available to anyone that wants to pay for it. That is, we will be able to see information and photographs about another country that have resolution on the order of yards or less, with obvious implications for local or even strategic warfare. The uses to which this information will be put will not always be benign.

Another closely related facet of this multidimensional picture of computer use is economic warfare. The ability to plan for, and respond to, economic crisis requires computers as a central tool. Recall, for example, the reallocation of oil that had to be carried out after the shock of the first oil embargo. That reallocation could not have been accomplished without extensive computer capability. Even the Iranian hostage negotiation involved computers. In order to reach agreement so that the hostages could be released on inauguration day, the use of an elaborate computer system in the banking community to transfer money rapidly was required.

Let me turn now to the effects of this technology on stability and the development of weapons, of their perceptions, and their use. There has been an increase in the complexity of weapons of war. Great glamour is attached in this country to designing and using weapons that are technically highly sophisticated. This is not so much the case in the Soviet Union, which is less enamored of complexity, preferring reliability. This movement toward greater complexity raises obvious questions of whether or not our systems will work when needed, of their vulnerability, and particularly of the maintenance and repair they require. It is a common observation that many of our sophisticated electronic and computer systems are not functioning when they are needed. Computers can be used to simplify complex systems and control them more easily and effectively. But the very complexities that the computers themselves lend to systems are a source of instability and uncertainty, especially with regard to performance reliability.

More directly, the role computers played in increasing accuracies of weapon systems had a substantially destabilizing effect on the strategic balance between the United States and the Soviet Union. The ability of intercontinental missiles to hit targets with great accuracy in effect jeopardizes another nation's fixed weapons systems, not just its cities. This is, of course, one of the requirements for a first-strike capability. Clearly, the development of computers was an essential element in bringing about that capability and its resulting danger. As long as weapons were relatively inaccurate, one could assume with confidence the survivability after attack of a retaliatory strike capability. A nation could threaten certain retaliation because its weapons could not be destroyed on the ground. As accuracy improved, the possibility arose that a retaliatory second strike could be prevented, which reduced the deterrent effect of a weapons system as a whole and created a premium for striking first. The United States has emphasized offensive weapons in several different modes—ground, sea, and air—whereas the Soviet Union has concentrated a larger fraction of its weapons on the ground, because of geographical position. The Soviet Union argued that a large number of multiple-warhead accurate missiles (an example of combining computers with another technology) could destroy Soviet ground missiles before they could be launched. The Soviet Union thus perceived that we were developing a first-strike capability, and that development was destabilizing because it threatened their deterrent. We argued that we were simply increasing the number of our missiles, so that in case of a Soviet attack, we would be able to retaliate. Which view prevails depends in part on where you are sitting, but from an analytical point of view, it is clear that in this case accuracy leads to instability. To recreate some stability, one possibility would be to build more sea-based weapons which can not be knocked out by high-accuracy systems since the exact location of sea-based systems is less likely to be known.

If we or the Soviet Union had an antiballistic (ABM) system, it, too, would increase world instability. That is, if it were possible to defend against a high proportion of incoming missiles, then, in one sense, land-based missiles could be protected, which would add to deterrent strength by protecting retaliatory capability. However, in another sense, it means that a nation has an incentive to attack first, thus limiting the retaliatory attack its ABM system must cope with. The ability to reduce retaliatory damage undermines the keystone of deterrence.

In general, the dependence of R&D on computers and related systems has a potentially destabilizing effect; it can, in fact, be argued that R&D as a whole has a destabilizing effect on the international structure. For example, one characteristic of arms-control agreements is that it is usually current capabilities that are being dealt with and not what will be in existence in ten or twenty years. Consequently, continued R&D that alters current capabilities tends to subvert existing arms-control agreements.

With regard to computer developments, continued R&D is likely to create situations that change what may be a relatively stable balanced situation. Consider, for example, the delivery time of weapons. If weapons were delivered by aircraft, there would be a clear understanding of what was required to launch an attack and a fairly clear assessment of vulnerability, preparation time for a potential attack, and how to respond. This understanding yields a reasonable stability to the situation. With a variety of delivery systems, some with extremely short delivery times, and with computers to coordinate timing in order to achieve maximum impact, the situation becomes less predictable, much more volatile and requires quick, even instantaneous, response decisions and is thus much less stable. By being an essential part of such a delivery system computers can be said to cause the instability.

It could be argued, on the other hand, that because computers have such rapid information-processing capabilities, they are a match for the short delivery times of existing weapons systems. The prompt real-time analysis of data, in fact, makes possible human decision rather than a preprogrammed response. That is, if it were not for the existence of large, rapid computers, we would have no choice but to build our weapons systems and design our strategy to respond to an indication of an attack rather than actual attack. This situation would be more dangerous and more unstable than one where there was at least an opportunity for human decision. High military officials are, however, active proponents of some sort of "strike on warning." They believe we should design retaliatory systems so that they would be fired automatically without Presidential decision if there is a computer warning of attack. This country, in my view, fortunately does not have that system. Nevertheless, there is an active element in the military and in the civilian sector that would like to see a strike on warning procedure put into effect. The Russians have also threatened adopting such a doctrine if NATO emplaces very short time-to-target missiles in Europe.

One of the most disturbing uses of computers for me at least, and one which may pose the greatest danger is in the area of planning, tactics, and strategy training. Here the problems and dangers are associated with computer models, the simulation process, and their role in decision making. One unavoidable problem associated with construction of a model is that certain assumptions are built into it. When the model is actually used, the assumptions are not easily accessible; in fact, by examining the output it is not generally possible to tell what assumptions were used. In addition, there is a general attitude that the more variables included in a model, the better and in some sense more credible the output must be. Presumably, the closer the model can come to approximating reality (more variables), the better it is. Unfortunately, this attitude is not based on an understanding of either the complexity involved or the relationships among variables. It is often assumed, for example, that the relationships expressing interactions between variables are linear; however, they may be nonlinear, which means that a model based on linear relationships will be quite inadequate.

In military and strategic areas these problems become particularly disturbing. For example, there is a tendency in model building to deal with everything quantitatively. The emphasis on things that can be measured—rather than the qualitative aspects of a situation—creates a large bias. The qualitative aspects are not dealt with because one cannot deal with them quantitatively. And so they are ignored, or left to be considered later, which usually means they are forgotten, especially when the printed outputs appear authoritative. There is also a tendency to include as much numerical data as possible in a model, not just what is important. The computer provides the capability for handling and collecting large amounts of data so there is little incentive to ask what data are actually needed, what is actually important for the question asked. And of course, models are vulnerable to conscious bias, which can assure the desired output from the beginning. It is quite likely that individual models of the same situation built by the air force, navy, and army will each indicate that its own service is entitled to more money for more weapons or more whatever, despite the fact that all three are modeling exactly the same situation.

The result of all this is a loss of wisdom and loss of the ability to think. In the military/strategic area too often there is a substitution of computer programs for the use of common sense. One of the questions asked Mr. Andersen was whether computers and computer models might not preempt thoughtful decisions and lead to automatic ones that would be absurd. Mr. Andersen's very moderate and sensible response was that results from a model that don't conform to common sense should be thrown out. I agree with that but it doesn't happen, at least it doesn't happen in these security areas. There is too much pressure; the situation is intimidating. The models are very complex; the assumptions are not well expressed; relationships are hidden; the situation is unfamiliar. Who can challenge the system? The system has responded. How is one individual able to say that this really does not seem right? (See question

25 and responses.) There is no space for the human element in this situation. On numerous occasions, both in Washington and in the classroom, I have seen situations where people are exposed to role-making for research purposes or perhaps for training purposes, and the participants come out believing what they have just seen. That is, participants have a strong sense that the model has simulated the way world events would happen if that particular scenario were to unfold. Wargames and simulation are used in the Pentagon frequently for sensitizing military and others to particular situations, and they are very believable. They are credible; I would argue, too credible, too believable. People come out not thinking they've just participated in a research exercise or even in a training exercise; they come out believing they've experienced reality and that's how it would be if the flag went up and suddenly we were at war.

At the present time within our government, we are faced with an estimate of our strategic situation based on a calculation generally accepted by the nation and the world. It is the question of Russia's capability compared to the West's in intercontinental missiles and strategic weapons. The Russians are believed to have achieved parity in strategic forces, and to be able to forge ahead; the popular conception is that very early in the 80s, the Russians will be able to launch a first strike and simply destroy the United States. We will be unable to respond; more precisely, we do not have sufficient forces for a credible deterrent.

This view is based on intelligence information fed into strategic models of military capabilities and nuclear exchanges. It is based on calculations by very elaborate computer systems that deal with numbers of weapons and their capabilities. Some of these figures are clear, some are not; enough figures are probably known to complete the models. However, because they cannot be dealt with adequately, the models omit the uncertainties associated with operational performance, political decisions, and the actual development or unraveling of a real situation.

Whether such computer models are necessary and useful aids to broader analysis is entirely beside the point. Political leaders accept and act on these models, and it is difficult for anyone to voice skepticism about the models. There is an enormous sense of intimidation involved. It's not formal or actual or intended intimidation. These are almost all honorable people with no intent to deceive. But the process is one in which somebody coming into office in the Pentagon is not basically in a position to challenge the output from models of these kinds. The calculations are presented as fact, and they have to be treated that way. We need computer systems and the information they produce, but somehow their limitations must be recognized more effectively than they are at present. It may be a matter of overriding importance.

Although this issue is the most important, the most disturbing, to me, there are other topics that relate directly to stability. Highly complex computer systems may be vulnerable to espionage of an esoteric kind; infiltration of the command and control systems would have effects that are difficult to predict. Complex systems are vulnerable to breakdown. Presumably computers can make it easy to build redundancy in systems; still, there are possibilities of breakdown that we cannot respond to quickly. There are opportunities for direct and overt system misuse. The illegal bombing of Cambodia during the Vietnam war was listed on computer printouts as Vietnam. Above a particular operational level, computers were simply programmed to show that bombing strikes were taking place in Vietnam. And there is the possibility of misinformation and misinterpretation, such as the supposed atomic explosion off South Africa in 1980. Initially the data collected by the satellite was interpreted as being associated with the explosion of an atomic weapon. Concurrent evidence in the South Pacific and Chile, contributed to that conviction. However, the evidence from both sources turned out to be false.

Finally, I cannot help but be concerned about the number of traditional areas of our economy and society which can become military and strategic issues. (See question 27 and responses.) Because of our growing ability both to know what is going on in those subjects very broadly, and our growing ability to control them, they are of increasing strategic importance. Food, resources, and weather are clearly in this category. Interdependence is the key word in planning, and computers have become a fundamental resource in planning. This situation raises grave dangers of misjudgment, of sacrificing real political and human control, of making the wrong assumptions and focusing only on what is measurable. Even in military areas, the sheer complexity of military weapons and operations guarantees enormous interdependence of aspects of these systems. A significant change in one aspect could have an enormous ripple effect. There is danger, too, in the use of computers that would encourage more technocratic decision-making both in military and civilian areas. The role of the computer, in effect, often denies or makes more difficult public participation and control in critical areas.

Computers are not necessarily different from other technologies that have the potential for good and bad results. However, computers, more so than most technologies, create dangers not easily understood by those they affect, because computers require a high level of sophistication and knowledge to interpret what is going on and what is going into them. By their very nature, then, computers would seem to pose more serious problems than other technologies. Certainly, computers are an integral part of security measures and have a major effect on international stability. And their role can only grow.

8. *Privacy, Technology, and Regulation*

ALAN F. WESTIN

Whenever the topic of computers and privacy or computers and personal freedom or personal information and technology is discussed, very quickly two rather starkly competing views are expressed. On the one hand are the shimmering optimists, who look at the arrival of a new technology—for example, an information technology—and see only benefits. They imagine that this technology has the enormous capacity to release mankind from the controls of nature and from the limitations on the use of information for making rational decisions in organizations. It will assist in achieving a true understanding of social problems and it will be of value in tailoring a variety of services to all of the individual interests and specialties of us as people, as consumers, as patients, as individuals who want to engage in various kinds of creative and specialized activities. Those who take the optimistic view see the computer as a colossal breakthrough in the available power to make benign decisions by organizations and by government which is aimed really at the freeing of individuals from a variety of limitations. So one stream of the literature looks at the computer as a means toward freedom. It sees the computer as a technique or a set of available tools that makes possible a variety of tasks that previously were not even imagined.

At the opposite end of the pole is the Orwellian nightmare. Information technology, computers, communications systems, and allied equipment will make it possible for organizations of social control, government, or employers or a variety of monitoring agencies to gather quantities of information about the individual, to put together a highly detailed picture of the individual's past and present activities. All of the anonymity and spontaneity and all of the capacity to avoid that kind of total monitoring and surveillance is suddenly in danger of being lost to us. In the Orwellian nightmare, computers offer the possibility for social control, jeopardizing the very foundation on which individual freedom has been built in Western democratic and constitutional states.

Let us review twenty-five years of computer use and development in the United States since roughly the late 1950s—when computer systems began to be widely used in record keeping by government, business, and the private sector—to the present. It is important to do this in order to determine which elements of the optimistic vision and which elements of the Orwellian nightmare seem to emerge as credible and important concerns that we should be worried about and which ones are fantasies that I believe we can dismiss as worries that people had or assumptions that people made that have been put to rest by experience and by better understanding.

The first step is to paint the base line, to look at the American approach to privacy and the organizational use of information in what could be called the precomputer era. There are a number of assumptions from this period that frame the way in which American society and law and technology approached issues of privacy and issues of technological development. According to our eighteenth-century constitutional heritage, while freedom and liberty and autonomy were important, they were never absolute in an ordered society. That is, our Bill of Rights and our concepts of individual liberty assumed that freedom of speech and freedom of press and religious liberty and other aspects of our freedom were vital to the development of autonomous individuals and organizations. These independent entities had the right to criticize government and suggest ways of limiting governmental abuse of power. However, concerns for order and legality meant that there were times when free speech could be limited and the press could be limited. There were times when religious claims to do things in the name of religious liberty had to be rejected because of concerns as to public health or concerns about the safety of minors or about offending public morals, for example. There was always a notion of balance, of equilibrium, in the way we regarded claims of liberty vs. claims of order or authority.

If we look at the Fourth Amendment to the Constitution, for example, which grants the right of citizens to be secure in their person, home, papers, and effects against unreasonable search and seizure, we see that the only direct statement related to personal privacy refers to unreasonable search and seizure. The Constitution does not grant the right to be totally free from any intrusion by government into private places or private papers. When the Fourth Amendment defined what was unreasonable, it stated that warrants to search or seize should be issued only when there was probable cause for believing that a crime had been committed or was about to be committed. The demonstration of probable cause had to be made before an independent magistrate or judge, who would weigh the claims for intrusion againt the need to protect personal and group privacy.

Other parts of the Constitution had helped to elaborate the structure of our ideas of privacy. The Fifth Amendment, providing that the individual did not have to give testimony against himself, was based on our reaction against compulsory disclosure in proceedings and testimony. For example, the requirement that there be no religious test for office was a way of trying to prevent individuals from having to confess their religious beliefs in order to serve in public life. As far as other aspects by which the classic American legal approach attempted to deal with privacy, much of it was rested upon what could be called the existential conditions by which people could try to protect reasonably their right to communicate and their right to withhold.

Because eavesdropping in the day of Blackstone or Jefferson meant lurking under the eaves of a house to listen to a conversation taking place inside, the very approach to privacy in the Constitution was based on the assumption, technologically correct at the time, that the only way of learning what was going on in people's homes or offices was to intrude physically into them.

Our law built our concept of privacy around the idea that people could not physically intrude into protected places unless they satisfied the warrant requirement and a judge had a chance to pass on the reasonableness of the intrusion. In response to the creation and development of the telephone, telegraph, and microphone, American law attempted to maintain that original balance. Antitelephone- and antitelegraph-tapping statutes did develop, but none of these statutes gave absolute immunity to the use of the telephone or the telegraph. The statutes included information about requirements for getting warrants or providing means of protecting in the normal course the privacy of those means, of the new technology, communication.

One other aspect that was quite important was the combination of living pattern and technological limitation that controlled or that surrounded our approach to record keeping and data on people. Unlike European monarchies that we rebelled against in creating the United States, we did not believe in police permits, registration of people in local communities, or the showing of identity papers when one checked into an inn or a hotel. We made a great deal of the fact that one could go west and take a new name and create a new identity. The American experience as we filled out the continent and as people fled from earlier lives and experiences in Europe and elsewhere gave us a tremendous bias against the kind of identification and dossier-record systems that were so much a part of European life from the days of monarchies to the rise of early nation-states and in autocratic and eventually totalitarian regimes in Europe. Thus, the United States never had an identity card, a registration or permit system, and while we paid some price for this, perhaps—for instance, in terms of someone being able to assume a new identity for purposes of fraud—it was considered to be a small price for the sense of liberation and freedom that came with the American experience. The kind of nation we were, the kind of problems that we faced all made us feel that this was the right way to approach records and privacy in America.

This brings us to the very late 1950s and early 1960s, the era of first or early alarms. What was significant about this period was not just the computer, but the awareness on the part of a number of social commentators and social observers that a number of new technological developments seemed to be threatening, if not shattering, the equilibrium that had previously been established between social values, law, and technological opportunity.

There were three areas in which commentators noted things were changing rapidly and somewhat menacingly. The first was in the area of physical-surveillance capabilities. The arrival of microminiaturization and a variety of developments in acoustics now made eavesdropping possible in ways that had never existed before. Detecting mechanical vibrations from such structures as windows and thin partitions made it possible to listen to conversations inside houses or offices without necessarily having to trespass physically. And camera technology made it possible to photograph people from extraordinary distances and often to obtain images in virtual darkness through infrared photographic techniques. It became possible to overhear conversations in the proverbial rowboat in the middle of Central Park or in the middle of a football field with the parabolic microphone. What had happened was that the walls and windows which had been the anchor for the theory of privacy and for the way in which intrusion into privacy was defined and either prevented or moderated had been overtaken by the new technologies of eavesdropping and of photography. As a result, to the extent that law required physical trespass, it was rendered obsolete by new technology.

And far from being a technology available to only the CIA or the rich and powerful forces in the society, the early 1960s saw so much of this equipment in local stores that the advantage appeared to have shifted to the would-be eavesdropper or voyeur. What had perhaps originally started out as wartime or cold-war technology had now reached the stage of general consumer production.

A second area of concern in this early period was psychological surveillance. New techniques were developed to determine whether or not somebody was telling the truth through devices that no longer require the individuals be directly in contact with the device. A device emerged in the early 1960s that surreptitiously photographed the blink rate of the eye and used that as a measure of stress in order to make judgments about truth or falsity. The psychological stress evaluator (PSE) recorded the voice and then examined changes in frequency modulation in order to determine if the subject was lying. The assumption was that control over the changes of the frequency modulation of the voice are not subject to conscious control. A trained reader could supposedly look at a graph from the PSE and make correct judgments. Incidentally, developers of this device claimed they used it to check frequency modulations of the voices of the participants in the show "To Tell the Truth." For 98 or 99 percent of these shows, they were able to tell immediately who was the real person by simply listening to participants' voices in the opening statement.

Incidentally, I was doing some work with this device just about the time of Watergate. I suggested this might be a great way to find out if Richard Nixon was telling the truth when he was appearing at press conferences during his presidency saying he did not know anything about Watergate. A friend of mine who was a reporter for the London Sunday *Times* actually paid $3,000 for this machine and was trained to operate it. He put President Nixon's various press conferences through the machine. Unfortunately, he received indecisive readings. When he went back to the developers of the machine and asked for some explanation, they said the machine essentially requires that the individual have a conscious knowledge of whether or not he is telling the truth. If someone is literally incapable of knowing when he is lying, the machine cannot come up with a useful reading. That may or may not have been the explanation for why Richard Nixon's comments never proved measurable on the PSE Device.

In addition to these forms of psychological surveillance, new personality tests, originally designed for therapeutic and voluntary-counseling purposes, tests with questions about orthodoxy and unorthodoxy, conformity, religious belief, personal values, and sexual predilections were widely used in industry and government in the 1960s to make employment decisions. There was even some work being done at that time with LSD and other drugs. Washington was, in fact, caught up with the idea that there might, indeed, be some new family of drugs that would make it possible to achieve the ultimate dream of the intelligence services—the little vial that when surreptitiously dropped into the coffee of the person being questioned somehow rendered that person unable to lie. Much work was done in this area, some of it with terrible results in people's lives.

The following incident is one illustration of the attitude described above. When I was working on the issue, I went to Washington with a lawyer who was the head of the committee I was working with, The Association of the Bar of the City of New York. We met with a scientist from the National Security Administration who believed passionately that a miracle truth drug was the way in which worldwide disarmament and peace could be attained. His vision was that if only we could really develop this colorless and tasteless liquid then we would have the necessary control. For example, imagine a meeting at which Kennedy would be on one side of the table and Khrushchev would be on the other side. You drop some of the liquid in each one's glass and after they've tasted you'd say, "Have you tested any nuclear weapons in the last year?" They would be powerless to do anything but tell you the truth. The lawyer I was with, who was a well-seasoned diplomatic as well as commercial lawyer said, "But, sir, hadn't it occurred to you that if you ever achieve that system, they just wouldn't tell Kennedy and Khrushchev what had been done and you wouldn't be able to really know from their responses what had been done?" The scientist thought for a moment and said, "Yes, I guess we're going to have to administer it rather widely."

Still another area of concern was brain-wave analysis. At the time, work was being done in which it seemed that by hooking up apparatus to the brain, one could tell, for example, whether an individual was looking at red or green or some other kinds of pattern. The vision of the researchers (or those funding the research) was much too optimistic, obviously. But the literature was astir with thoughts that perhaps it would be possible to monitor the brain to learn about certain kinds of emotional states or attitudes in such a manner that the individual would be either unaware of, or unable to prevent this search from taking place. What each of the psychological technologies that were being experimented with had in common was that in some way, they penetrated the psychological self of the individual. They either produced or threatened to produce a power on the part of people who would have access to such techniques and instruments and tests to force people to disclose things about themselves that they did not choose to disclose voluntarily.

What proved to be most important and most far reaching and in many ways, most typical of surveillance technology, was new capacities in record or data surveillance. In this case, it was the development of the computer, with its special ability to collect, store, process, and distribute information that seemed to upset some of the most important privacy protections which the limitations of science had helped to nurture. Suddenly it was possible to collect so much more information about individuals, to analyze it, distribute it, exchange it, and to monitor on a real time basis what people were doing, where they were, what their transactions were and so forth. It seemed as if all of the protection of privacy that had lain in the limitations of armies of clerks and mountains of physical paper records, making limited the ability of government to collect and monitor large numbers of people, or large segments of the population, was in jeopardy. So in the area of data surveillance, the feeling was that suddenly all of the compartments within which we gave our information voluntarily for a given purpose—to medicine, to education, to government for licensing or benefits, to law enforcement investigations—that all of the walls between those compartments in which we gave limited information were suddenly going to be swept away or electronically penetrated by the capacity of computer systems to amass all of that information or to exchange it among the compartment organizations on an immediate basis. And in response to this potential invasion of privacy, there were a number of books and articles, congressional hearings, and television programs from the early 1960s until about 1968 or 1969 that examined whether the age of privacy were dead. People wondered whether the arrival of these new technologies had resulted in new situations which by their very nature had gone beyond the legal concepts which had controlled the activities of powerful government and private organizations of the past. They wondered whether they had lost the capacity to bring these instruments of surveillance under the kind of limitation and control that had been characteristic of our society previously.

At this point, we enter the next phase, the period of empirical study and new conceptual development, when most Western parliamentary systems established expert commissions or government commissions to review the new technologies, especially in the computer area. They were to sort out what was fact from what was fantasy in terms of what the systems could do, what they were doing and to understand what kinds of capacities there might be to impose limits or to reimpose boundaries on these powerful new technologies. In the United States, for example, there was a study by the National Academy of Sciences, that I directed from the Computer Science and Engineering Board, which spent three years looking at how computers were actually being used by government agencies, private organizations, and commercial organizations. The Secretary's Advisory Committee on Automated Personal Data Systems, a committee set up by Secretary of HEW Elliot Richardson, considered what new legal and administrative concepts might address these issues of record keeping. In Britain, a committee was set up by Parliament to look at these issues, and in Sweden, a royal commission of a similar kind was set up. A number of countries in the Western parliamentary traditions held parallel inquiries searching after the reality of the new technology and its uses and to look at what kinds of interventions might make sense.

In the United States, the HEW Committee, for example, examined how American regulation had tried to deal with the use of information and power and noted that we had a concept of fair practices that had been widely used in American regulation. We had, for example, fair labor and fair trade practices. In 1970, in the first real piece of privacy legislation, we developed in the Fair Credit Reporting Act a similar concept about the use of credit reports to affect an individual's credit or employment or insurance opportunities.

Our approach to the problem of record keeping was to reveal record-keeping practices to individuals, give them access to their own records, and let them challenge completeness or accuracy. We did not want to get deeply into the issue of what information could be collected. We wanted people to have some control over the circulation of information relating to them.

There are two things about that that I think mark the way in which we implemented the understandings that came through in this period of empirical study and first concept formulation. The first was that we needed some political impetus in order to pass the necessary legislation. In addition, if there were going to be costs involved in trying to create rights in records systems and information, what would limit the expenses charged to the consumer or the taxpayer in creating these new systems to inform people of their rights and let them exercise such rights? It might well have been a good deal longer than it was before a country like ours enacted such legislation, were it not for the fact that one event took place that changed the whole calculus of action, and that event was Watergate.

When you stop to think about it: when historians in the year 2000 write about privacy and computers, they probably will say that the patron saint of the Federal Privacy Act of 1974 was indeed Richard Nixon. The reason was that Watergate was perceived by the articulate public in America and by the general public as being essentially about information. That is, it was the effort by the president and his supporters and his subordinates to acquire information in illegitimate ways, either by breaking and entering into a psychiatrist's office to get information on Daniel Ellsburg, or by trying to use IRS records to punish enemies, or to compile lists of enemies and circulate them throughout the government, or to engage in the "plumbers' operation" and other forms of breaking and entering, or Watergate itself, the entry into the Democratic Party's headquarters to plant listening devices on the telephones or the offices. Each of those elements that we call in shorthand Watergate, plus the lying and the attempt to cover up what had happened raised the question of illegitimate use of information by people in power. That this could happen in the precomputer era before information technology really took hold in the Federal establishment made a lot of people very concerned that new rules should be developed and new standards set before we reached the vast increase in information capability that the arrival of large-scale computer systems would mean in the Federal establishment and in government generally and in the private sector as computer technology expanded.

For those of us who were very interested in privacy and talked about the emerging issues of what needed to be done, there always was someone who would get up and say, "Well, that's all well and good but that's all potential, just show us anybody in authority in the good old U.S. of A. that would abuse their authority to collect and use information." After Watergate unraveled, that answer was very easy: Richard Nixon. This then provided the impetus to pass the Federal Privacy Act of 1974. (See question 24 and responses.)

The Act covers all federal agencies and departments and requires every agency to list publicly the records compiled about individuals whether they are licensees, government program beneficiaries, taxpayers, or veterans. Any time a federal department, agency, or bureau opens an identified personal record, it has to list and describe completely each system of records that it creates. Individuals have the right to know what information has been collected about them and they can demand to see what is in their record. There are a few exceptions for intelligence files and certain kinds of law enforcement files, but the Act is an extraordinarily general guarantee of the right of the individual to have knowledge of, and access to, information that federal agencies collect. There is an important section that says that unless specifically authorized by Congress, no information can be collected and stored about an individual by a federal agency concerning the exercise of First Amendment rights, that is, rights of speech, press, association, religion, and so forth.

The second point that seems important about the way in which we made our first attempt at creating a new balance between information technology and privacy is that we consciously rejected what came to be the European model of what to do about this issue. When, as I mentioned, other countries such as the Continental nations—Sweden, West Germany, France, the Netherlands, and others—held similar inquiries and developed commissions and reports, they chose a very different approach. They chose one that is deep in the Napoleonic Code tradition and reflects the political cultures of European states. They created a registrar, or data-commission system, to protect privacy from computers and high technology. Sweden was the first country to pass such a national data-protection law in 1973, and seven other European countries now have very similar statutes. Essentially, these laws provide that before any organization, government agency, or corporation can create a computer system containing identified personal records, it must apply for a license from the data protection commission, which sets general standards for security, confidentiality, access, and so forth. The commission examines the record system to certify whether or not it is acceptable. Citizens can complain to the data protection commission if they cannot see their record or their privacy is being abused, and the data protection commission will investigate. The Swedish data protection commission consists of people appointed from government, trade unions, business, education, professions, and so forth.

What is striking about this European approach is it gives the government control over the use of computer technology in society. In some ways the countries have been, we might say, "puritanical" about their approach to what can and can't be done. For example, the Swedes have refused to allow the licensing of computer dating bureaus. Their attitude is that it creates too much dangerous information about personal dimensions of life and therefore it is not acceptable, whereas the American approach has been that such systems are accepted and allowed to operate as a matter of free enterprise. If there is an abuse shown—blackmail or the selling of names in ways that people don't approve—then we would use criminal prosecution or we would invoke other kinds of protection such as the right to see what they record about you rather than assuming that we will not allow such a use of computers to take place. The idea of European data commissions is very much in keeping with trust in government and high confidence in the administrative state. This approach is a part of the Continental European legal tradition.

One thing that helps to show why Americans have approached this problem differently is to imagine what would have happened if we had had such a data protection commission in the United States in 1973. It is obvious that someone like Charles Colson would have been chairman of the commission, and someone like John Dean would have been its general counsel. Since they would have been familiar with all the locks and keys and security measures, they would probably have had more knowledge and control over circulation and movement in the country than any one else.

The Federal Privacy Act of 1974 recognized that it had dealt only with the federal government, and so it provided for the creation of a federal commission. This Privacy Protection Study Commission, a two-year research body, was to look into whether the principles of the Federal Privacy Act should be applied to the private sector in banking, credit cards, employment, medical records, insurance, and also among state and local governments. While the Commission held a series of hearings, eight or nine states passed statutes similar to the Federal Privacy Act, providing that state and local government agencies would follow the same laws pertaining of fair information practices. The Privacy Commission then signaled the need for legislation to establish the same principles of fair information practice for private areas as in the federal sector.

The Carter administration after a year and a half of rather slow digestion recommended many of these ideas in what was known as the Carter Privacy Package, which was presented to Congress in early 1979. What happened to that package is rather instructive. Some of it passed rather quickly; for example, even before the whole package was presented, the Financial Right to Privacy Act of 1978 was passed. The reason for this prompt passage was an earlier Supreme Court decision in the Miller Case, which ruled that an individual does not have a constitutional right to privacy with regard to his bank account.

Neither checking accounts nor savings accounts in a bank are secure. The bank cannot object if the government comes and wants to look at someone's financial records. The individual does not have to be notified and has no right that can be asserted at that point to try to prevent the authorities from going through bank records on the ground that the subpoena is invalid or the search is too broad or other defenses one has if you have a claim that the law will recognize to privacy. What the Supreme Court said was that because you had revealed the information to the bank you had lost your reasonable expectation to privacy. Even though the banker had the duty of confidentiality to you, the government could simply, anytime it wanted to, get your bank records. Well, touching bank accounts touches the heart of capitalist society and it didn't take very long before a strange alliance of the American Bankers Association, the ACLU, *Nation* magazine, and the *Wall Street Journal* were crusading together for privacy-protection legislation for financial records. The point was that our financial records are, indeed, a documentation of our transactions in society. There was a clear sense that this was an important part of transactional privacy that needed some protection so Congress did pass a good statute, the Financial Right to Privacy Act in 1978.

But the Financial Right to Privacy Act is actually the only piece of legislation stemming from the Privacy Commission's recommendations and the Carter administration's recommendations approved by Congress. A medical privacy act, which looked as if it were going to pass, was lost at the last minute in the waning hours of the Carter administration, largely because of a sudden and unexpected claim by intelligence agencies that they wouldn't be able to obtain the doctors' and medical records they needed. A bill providing protection of insurance privacy—

that is, privacy for individuals in their application for life or health insurance or auto insurance and in the claims process—was also recommended by the Carter administration. This bill failed to pass because the insurance industry and business resisted federal regulation as opposed to state fair-insurance-information laws.

Where does this leave us then in the 1980s? First, we have learned that computers can do very little of what some of the four-color brochures and promotional touting of technological enthusiasts promised. Also, the market functions as a control mechanism on the adoption of potential computer technologies and deserves our continued respect. That is, much of what could be done by computers will be done on a large scale in the United States only if someone can make a great deal of money from it or if the government is willing to pay for it. All the assumptions that people made in the late 1960s—for example, that very quickly we would go to a checkless, cashless society where one piece of plastic would buy in the grocery store, would pay for our magazine subscriptions, the bus, and the parking lot—did not include one essential point. While all this is technologically feasible in an abstract sense, it is awesomely expensive and, therefore, tied to the market mechanism of who would want this and who would pay for it. The fear in the 1960s that with computers, information would be collected and distributed automatically without the individual's knowledge turned out to be unfounded. Software is much more complicated than had been anticipated. Information is a power resource that nobody gives freely. We can set boundaries and can control access in very, very effective ways. In addition, it is important to realize that in the pre-computer era things were not so rosy. We can actually improve information control and responsibility in many ways with a well-organized computer system. We can, therefore, often give greater protection to information in a computer system than in the highly decentralized, leaky manual-record era in many situations. (See question 26 and responses.)

Second, we have had to decide how much to intervene in the use of information in society, why to intervene, and how to intervene if we are going to maintain the balance that our democratic society had worked out between information and privacy before the computer era.

The computer arrived in the 1960s and 1970s, when we were undergoing a social revolution about who was entitled to enjoy the benefits and opportunities of American society. The equality movement demanded that previous records systems of dossiers containing discriminations against people could not be allowed to continue, which meant that such information could not be entrusted to new computer systems that would make dissemination of discriminatory judgments even more effective. Thus, our reaction to the computer was influenced by the fact that we were undergoing a transformation of values and opportunities in our society. The computer had to be disciplined to serve our social purposes, and not allowed to incorporate earlier biases.

Third, we have had to come to grips with the question of how much we want to intervene to change the power distributions in society as a result of questions of privacy and fair information practices. There are still two opposing views on how to protect privacy from computer abuse. The fair-information-practices approach wants systems to operate as they are today, at the discretion of the large organizations controlling computer technology. But to curtail information abuse, individuals have been given access to that information. Another approach argues that we have allowed computer technology to unfold in a way that enforces already existing power structures in society. Unlike the Molotov cocktail, a power redistributing technology which is inexpensive, a computer system is very costly to construct, purchase, and operate. It requires armies of highly trained and paid officials to run and service it. So computer technology has tended to enhance the existing power structures in the society. Whether that is the proper course or not is a social question that obviously we have to debate as a society. So far, however, the question of redistributing power resources through information control has not been part of the American response to computer-technology control.

To close, let me just suggest that there is one person's life I think embodies the best of the approach that we ought to take as our ideal here. Thomas Jefferson was a man who had an equal commitment to science and to freedom. In his day he was one of the great scientists and writers about science. He was an inventor and an applied technologist. He was someone who believed that science could open up new opportunities and possibilities for the human race so that we could conquer the controls and limits of nature. On the other hand, he understood power and its abuse. He understood the potentialities of the human spirit and of individuality and freedom; he was always concerned that we limit the potential abuses of power and that we provide systems of checks and balances so that rights and liberties are not abused. For him it was not science or freedom, it was really the highest art of the American approach to try to find a way to have both. Trying to establish a balance between the advantages of scientific and technological progress and a commitment to individual freedom was the essence of the American Republic. That is the kind of ideal that we still need in order to determine how to balance the resources of information technology in a democratic society. I think that Jefferson offers us the approach and the commitment that ought to be our approach today.

9. *Questions and Replies*

Eugene B. Skolnikoff and Alan F. Westin

Question 24: Under the credit law, people asking for a credit rating are informed of an investigation if such is required; is there a similar requirement for the Federal Privacy Act?

Westin: No, they are different systems. According to the Fair Credit Reporting Act, a corporation preparing an investigative report on someone must state that it is going to generate such a report. Then if denied insurance or employment because of that report, the individual can ask to see the report. It would have been both impractical and a kind of ecological disaster to have assumed in law that every time a federal agency collected information about you it had to notify you. According to the Federal Privacy Act, every federal department and agency has to list publicly its records on individuals, who then have the right to know what information has been collected about them. Some people suggested that any time a government agency opened a file on an individual, that individual would have to be notified and would have a right to see what was going to be put in the file before it happened. That is an extraordinarily impractical and costly way to go about it. If an individual is denied something or if in some way he is harmed, let the individual decide whether he wants to see what is in there. This is a much more practical way to give rights without creating the administrative nightmare of the other approach.

Question 25: Professor Skolnikoff, you stated that it is very difficult for a politician to challenge conclusions based on computer-assisted projections. In addition, Professor Andersen expressed concern about models and decision making. He mentioned the problem of faulty assumptions built into models and the situation where there isn't time or perhaps the resources to analyze results. This is especially important, of course, when rapid decision making is required. Would you expound a little on how we can challenge various policy decisions?

Skolnikoff: The problem I was referring to is not faced solely by politicians. The whole environment an office holder experiences when he comes into a large organization, into a kind of subculture, is such that he is surrounded basically with one general point of view (obviously there are many different points of view, but in general, a whole environment leading in one direction). The office holder is presented with data, outputs of models, and calculations. He just doesn't have the time to challenge the results even if he were so inclined. Often there is no reason to suspect that there is any need to challenge the results, especially when he is in an environment which doesn't lead him to suspect that there might be other answers. We're all subject to that; it's not peculiar to the Pentagon. All our views are heavily influenced by where we happen to be sitting, in any field, whether it's military or environmental or university or consumer oriented or whatever. It is difficult psychologically for anyone to enter an environment (and computers have nothing to do with this) and challenge the prevailing wisdom of that environment. In addition, when an existing information or analytical system is heavily dependent on calculations or information not readily accessible to the individual, even with all the time in the world, there isn't much he would do. Everything militates against his challenging those conclusions. Therefore, it is important for society to have institutions outside the government with sources of information and analytical expertise that can balance what is inside the government. This is particularly difficult in military security or in other areas where one has classification to deal with. The people on the outside need either to have access to classified information or at least to have had access at some point in the not too distant past. This saves those outside from being easily defeated just by having someone in government say, well, you don't have access to all the information (a useful tactic). In any case, there is a need for having the capability to challenge the government's expertise on a roughly equal basis.

Question 26: I had expected Professor Westin's conclusions to be more negative or pessimistic, but it seems that we really don't have too much to worry about in terms of loss of privacy. Is that a fair conclusion?

Westin: A number of positive results have been achieved. However, this required the mobilization of privacy-minded groups in the society and a sensitizing of the American public to the importance of privacy and the need to control information abuse. A political climate was created in the sixties and seventies that enabled us to insist that managers of computer systems voluntarily institute information-abuse controls. This didn't happen just because divine providence smiled on us or because this kind of thing was somehow built into the logic of our party politics. It was an achievement that required political struggle and education, as did civil rights and women's rights. As long as this perspective is not lost, I can be somewhat optimistic in the eighties.

As long as we keep on struggling, pointing out the potential abuses of a whole host of new federal information systems for the IRS or the Social Security Administration; as long as we are skeptical about creating a worker's identity card, we will not be caught unaware. If we keep in mind that cable television, two-way communications systems, or electronic fund-transfer plans are potentially dangerous and require safeguards, we will be able to combine technical innovation with security and confidentiality concerns. I am also optimistic on this issue because all the public opinion studies, including a very elaborate national study done in 1979, have shown an interesting marriage between the liberal political and the strong conservative viewpoints on limiting information abuse by both government and the private sector.

Question 27: Professor Skolnikoff, would you agree that the limitations of a one-sided analysis in military thinking points to the need for an interdisciplinary or a more political approach to our problem solving and decision making?

Skolnikoff: Many of these issues can not be looked at wholly as one discipline or another, which doesn't mean that everything can be looked at only as interdisciplinary. Certainly, the program with which I am associated at M.I.T. in the political science department and also the one that I direct at the center aren't exactly that. The political science program called Science and Public Policy, attempts to train people from diverse backgrounds to deal with issues that cross traditional boundaries. At the center, we have research programs focusing on international impact or international issues raised by energy or communications or environmental or other technical issues. I believe very strongly in this approach, and I have spent a fair amount of time in Washington working with various offices and particularly the White House Science Office. There, the people who tend to be the most effective in dealing on a daily basis with the issues that we are discussing are those who have some kind of mixed training.

Question 28: Professor Westin, what is the relationship of the legislative process to protection as far as technological advances are concerned?

Westin: I don't see anything on the horizon in technology that overarches the basic concepts that we worked out in the seventies to provide protection in information-rich environments. No matter what the development, I do not see anything nullifying the concept that you can't open a record about somebody and make decisions about him without his knowledge, without the publication of it, that people have a right to control whether information that they give for one purpose is given to others and used for other purposes. In other words, the basic concepts of privacy or fair-information practice will have to be applied in each new technological context. I don't want to minimize the fact that there will be important choices for society to make about the new technology. For example, we are clearly moving toward more electronic funds transfer, which means that there will be two competing interests. One, the privacy interest, will not want elaborate records on individuals in such a transaction system. Unfortunately, there will be a need for legal authentication, account verification, fraud control, and so forth. The right balance will have to be found. There doesn't seem to me to be a technological breakthrough that we cannot handle; there will simply be value judgements to make.

Question 29: While the individual may have the right to find out what information has been gathered, would he know where or by whom? Whom would the individual question?

Westin: We still have known discrete record systems. We're not creating one national data bank on everybody and that's not going to happen in the eighties. Until we reach the point where we just don't know where the information originates and who is handling it and where it is going—a point that I do not think we will reach—we can handle the problem. I don't see any sign that information will be developed and used in society in the eighties in a traceless-gas-in-the-air kind of way. One of the interesting aspects of privacy is how much should be legislated for the whole society globally; how much should the computer be used to advance the basic claim of privacy, which is the right of individuals to decide what information is revealed and used about them. The nice thing about computer technology is that it can accommodate differences, can actually support the individual's own privacy boundary. We don't have to make those global choices.

Postscript: Computers and the Modeling of Mind

WARREN HOCKENOS

In a novel departure from early work in AI, Schank's work, like Minsky's, reflects the use of the computer to study the human mind. An early approach to AI, sometimes called the engineering approach, aimed solely at having the machine perform such difficult tasks as chess playing, problem solving, and theorem proving. But the programs were written with little regard for the manner in which humans performed the same task. Questions as to how people proved theorems, played chess or solved problems were simply not asked. The aim, primarily, was to have the machine do those "things that exhibit intelligence that are hard for even people to do," but not necessarily do them in the same way (Schank 1980, 2).

Minsky's work on frames and Schank's programs reflect a different set of theoretical concerns. The focal questions guiding their work are: How do people perform these cognitive tasks, and can we make the machine do them in the same way? This raises questions of a peculiarly philosophical or psychological sort: What kind of knowledge do people have and how is this knowledge used in order to perform the task at hand whether it is solving a problem or understanding a spoken or written sentence?

With this *problematik* in mind, the computer is not merely an engineering feat whose extraordinary capacities can be used to perform complicated tasks; rather, given the right program, what the computer does is thought to be identical with what the human mind does when it performs its various cognitive tasks. Conversely, when the human mind performs its cognitive tasks, it does so in the same way as a properly programmed digital computer.

The purpose of writing language-comprehension programs is, according to Schank, "to model human cognitive processes" (Schank 1972).

The programs SAM and PAM, model the cognitive ability of a person to understand simple stories and answer questions about goals, motives, and roles of agents in the story. Thus, the discipline of AI is not only a branch of cognitive psychology, but the programs themselves serve as explanations of psychological processes underlying the performance of various cognitive tasks. Advocates of this psychological approach to AI claim that in this question and answer sequence, the machine does not merely simulate a human being's ability but rather that the machine, in providing answers to questions about agents in the story, can literally be said to understand the story. Furthermore, the program itself instantiates a theory of human language understanding, and as a consequence, the program, as an instantiated theory, explains the human ability to understand the story and answer questions about it.

A first step in getting machines to think and understand sentences as we do is to provide as explicit a statement as possible of what goes on in our minds when we understand what another person is saying. The first step, therefore, is a theoretical one and requires answers to a variety of theoretical questions of which the following are representative. Since sentences in a natural language have a rich grammatical structure, how is this structure to be analyzed and represented? What contribution does this grammatical structure make to the meaning of a sentence? What role does our understanding of the semantic or meaning content play in parsing incoming sentences? How is the semantic dimension of sentences represented in the mind? What is the semantic dimension of a sentence, and what are the properties of words that give rise to it? Does each word and its meaning require a different symbolic form? How is our knowledge of the world represented, and what role does it play in our understanding of a natural language? What role does memory play, and how do we learn from the mistakes we make? A partial answer, at least, to such questions as these must be provided prior to writing a successful program.

This postscript focuses on a narrower range of questions having to do largely with the semantic or meaning dimension of language. Essential to any account of language, hence, *a fortiori*, to language comprehension, is an account of word and sentence meaning: What is it, and how is it processed or understood by the human mind? An abbreviated account of Schank's answer to this question takes the following form. Modeling his programs on what occurs in the human mind when communication is successful, Schank points to the fact that although we speak to one another in sentences, it is the meaning of those sentences and not the sentences themselves that is understood. Sentences, when construed as physical sounds or shapes (sometimes called inscriptions), vary from language to language, yet their meanings are often the same. The German sentence *es regnet*, though different in physical shape from the English *it is raining* and the French *il pleut*, means the same thing. This common meaning is the conceptual underpinning of each sentence that makes translation possible and forms the basis of our understanding. As Schank states, "The actual language output is merely an indicator of the conceptual content beneath it" (Schank 1972, 554).

Ambiguous sentences aside, each sentence has a unitary meaning or conceptualization that is not to be identified with the physical properties of the sentence itself. The source of this unitary sentence meaning is the concepts underlying the words or expressions formed from words; each word or sequence of words has a concept or set of concepts peculiar to it. The conceptual input of these various lexical items or expressions serve to produce the conceptual content of the sentence as a whole. Since this conceptual content is the same for all languages, it is interlingual or universal in character. Schank calls this the conceptual base. Thinking in a language is not a matter of thinking in sentences peculiar to that language, but, rather, in the universal conceptual base represented by the words and sentences of a natural language.

With the view that meaning underlies conceptualization, understanding a sentence seems to require a mental act that takes us from the sentence inscription to the underlying conceptualization. Schank suggests that understanding a sentence, whether in Greek, Hebrew, or English, occurs in a kind of translation process whereby the sentence in a natural language is translated into the interlingual conceptual base. This translation process is sometimes called a mapping and requires a set of mapping rules or translation algorithms by means of which the meaning of the English sentence is mapped into the conceptual base. The nature of these mapping rules is not altogether clear, but their necessity is obvious enough, and understanding results from that mapping.

To what extent can the above account serve as a semantic theory? Traditionally, semantics has been thought of as the discipline whose subject matter is, very broadly, word and sentence meaning. More specifically, a semantic theory tries to answer the questions: how is it possible for linguistic symbols to have meaning and how do words and sentences represent important properties of the world for the human mind. Those answers that have won the respect of professionals in the field attempt a careful specification of the relationship between language construed as symbols and the reality they symbolize. Language is thought to be symbolic in the sense that linguistic symbols represent the nonlinguistic world of stabbings, weddings, elections, toe-stubbings, eclipses, and fits of anger. By virtue of linguistic symbolization, we are able to symbolize nonlinguistic reality in such a way that it is possible to think and speak about the realm of the nonlinguistic with physical sounds and shapes alone. Some account of what enables such expressions as *is angry*, *is dying*, *is hitting*, and *is voting* to represent and convey moods, states, happenings, and activities is the subject of theoretical semantics. So construed, semantics accounts for the meaning of sentences and words by means of the relationship that such signs or symbols bear to what they designate. Only through some such relationship can linguistic symbols provide a representational device so that words serve as a surrogate for the reality talked and thought about.

Can Schank's notion of meaning as concept be interpreted as belonging to mainstream semantics? Not, it seems, without considerable revision, since Schank at no point concerns himself with the relationship between language and world. The fault does not lie with the theory of meaning construed as concept but, rather, with the fact that Schank has not used all of the resources available from some of the historical interpretations of this approach to meaning. A classical version of meaning as concept is that of John Locke, who construed the meaning of such general words as *horse* and *lead* to be names of abstract ideas in the mind. These abstract ideas serve as "bonds between particular things that exist and the names that they are to be ranked under" (Locke 1690). As a kind of mediator between word and world, abstract ideas are principles, procedures, or criteria for ranking things under general or sortal names. In this sense, knowing the abstract idea of *horse* or *lead* is tantamount to knowing "what are the alterations which may or may not be in a horse or lead, without making either of them to be of another species" (Locke 1690, 3.3.13). Put in somewhat more contemporary terminology, knowing the meaning of *horse* involves knowing what things are to be considered horses and what are not, as a consequence of knowing or possessing the abstract idea. To be able to identify the appropriate members of the class of horses is to know the extension of that class or the denotation of the general name *horse*.

Following Locke's insight, it would appear that the criteria for saying of someone that he knows the meaning of a general name are first, that he be able to identify those objects to which the name in question applies along with those things to which it does not apply; second, that the identifications which he makes correspond to those of other competent speakers in the community. In short, there must be a set of tacit semantic conventions that are recognized throughout the speech community with respect to the reference of the expression. If Schank were to regard concepts along Lockean lines as in some sense semantical rules determining the use or application of the word-token by establishing properties an object must have in order to be denoted by a particular word, it would place Schank in mainstream semantics. But Schank does not take advantage of these traditional resources.

It is worth looking at another account of this central semantic relationship between word and world in order to see what such a theory must provide to explain our understanding of a natural language. This account represents the traditional approach to semantics following a well-worn path trod by A. Tarski, G. Frege, R. Carnap, and, more recently, D. Davidson.

According to these semanticists, there is a close connection between meaning and truth. Earlier, it was noted that the pivotal idea in traditional semantics is that meaning is to be accounted for in terms of the way language relates to the world. The notion that truth sheds light on meaning exploits that insight. The point is, in order to understand the meaning of a sentence, we must first know what makes the sentence true. Consider the sentence *John hit Mary*. Normally, the sentence describes a particular happening or event. It could not be used, however, if it didn't mean that Mary was hit by John—exactly the condition that makes the sentence true. In other words, the condition rendering the sentence true is the sentence's meaning. That is, if I were to speak that sentence to another person, his understanding would depend on his knowing what is being described—knowing the kind of event or happening that makes the sentence true. Knowing the truth condition is tantamount to knowing the meaning of the sentence. Thus, when someone says *John hit Mary*, I understand it to the extent that I know what would be the case if the sentence were true. Of course, it need not necessarily be true. Thus, the truth condition of the sentence *New York City has a population of two million people* is a city of two million people, and that condition would have to be known in order to understand the meaning of the sentence. The sentence is, of course, false, but even if we didn't know that, we would understand its meaning by virtue of understanding those conditions that would prevail if it were true.

Truth conditions appear to be actual events or happenings in the world that make sentences true, but to so construe truth conditions is to misconstrue them. We understand many sentences, such as the one about New York City, whose truth condition, being a city of 2,000,000 people, isn't realized. Truth conditions are not particular events or happenings; they are abstract, like Locke's abstract ideas. Particular events make sentences true or false, but abstract truth conditions specify the kind of event or happening that has to occur for the sentence to be true. And those abstract conditions must be grasped if we are to understand the meaning of a sentence. Truth conditions, however, also leave something unexplained and somewhat mysterious, namely, what gives rise to them? Truth conditions are derived from a complicated set of conventions, both syntactical and semantical, governing word order and reference. By virtue of these conventions, sentences not only have truth conditions but represent the nonlinguistic world that we talk and think about. We now turn to these conventions.

Assuming the plausibility of the truth-condition account of sentence meaning, we may still legitimately ask about the contribution words composing a sentence make to sentence meaning in the sense of truth conditions. After all, nothing could be more obvious than the fact that the sentence *John kissed Mary* will have different truth conditions from *John hit Mary* and that the difference in truth conditions turns on the difference in meaning between the verbs *hit* and *kissed*. In addition, mastering a natural language entails learning the meaning of the vocabulary of that language: Producing new and unusual sentences can only be accomplished if we have mastered the necessary vocabulary and syntax. Our immediate concern is to delineate precisely how the meaning of words contributes to the meaning of a sentence construed as the truth condition.

The standard approach to this problem, called formal semantics, is Rudolph Carnap's, as first introduced in his monograph *The Foundations of Logic and Mathematics* in 1938. The conviction of such semanticists is that most of the vocabulary of a natural language has the meaning it does because of relationships these various lexical items bear to the world. Patterns of marks (word tokens, as they are sometimes called), such as *Roger Schank*, *hit*, *Mary*, *wise*, *turtle*, and so forth, mean what they do because of associations they have for us with things, properties of things, or happenings in the world. This is not to suggest that meanings of words are the things referred to. Meanings are not things. But words have meaning insofar as we associate them with space-time segments of both the physical and social environment. And truth conditions take root in these learned associations—words with things.

The proper function of a semantic theory is to provide a semantic interpretation for each and every sentence of the language by specifying their truth conditions. But the semantic interpretation of a sentence as a whole is a function of the semantic interpretation of its words. Nouns and noun phrases, for example, are interpreted by specifying things as their referents. Predicates are semantically interpreted by providing as referents sets of things having the property that the predicate denotes. For example, consider the sentence *Roger Schank is wise*; the proper name *Roger Schank* is interpreted by providing it with an assignment, namely, the person Roger Schank. This is called assigning an extension to a name; it is simply a more technical way of saying that *Roger Schank* denotes Roger Schank.

Similarly for predicates, the adjective *wise* is interpreted, that is, provided with a meaning by being assigned the set of individuals who are wise. The property of being wise is one that each and every member of the set of wise people has in common. Therefore, the predicate adjective *wise* is interpreted by reference to the set of individuals each of whom has that property.

Finally, the function of the copula verb *is* is to relate the referent of the noun phrase to the property expressed by the adjective. The copula *is* indicates that the individual who constitutes the extension of the noun phrase is included in the set of individuals that constitutes the extension of the adjective. Thus, the sentence *Roger Schank is wise* will be true if Roger Schank is a member of the set of things that are wise. In this fashion, conditions for the truth of the sentence are delineated by specifying those properties that the subject of the sentence must have in order for the sentence to be true. In order to be correctly described as understanding the sentence, we would have to know the truth conditions. In this sense, truth conditions are a direct function of the significant semantic properties of the words constituting the sentence and their syntactical organization. But most important for our criticism of Schank, the relevant semantic properties of words that produce truth conditions are the referential connections words have to the world by virtue of our semantic conventions.

By way of contrast to mainstream semantics, then, the Schankian program provides the following: first, the theory offers a strategy for mapping sentences into their conceptual base. The strategy, as we saw earlier, is to pair the sentence with a representation that is more revealing of conceptual content than its surface form alone. This paraphrase of the meaning of each sentence of the language into a formalism or representational notation that is interlingual distinguishes the underlying conceptualization from the sentence itself. Secondly, the translational process must be done algorithmically in the sense that some suitably general computational principles must associate each sentence with its appropriate conceptual representation. The theoretical principles providing this translation must also be specified in an unambiguous fashion. Finally, the theory providing the computational principles for mapping sentences into their canonical form must be construed as a model of what the speaker-hearer does when he understands a sentence. The program is, in effect, an instantiation of a theory of how human beings understand sentences. Thus, when the system (computer plus program) paraphrases sentences into the interlingual symbolism, it can literally be said to understand the meaning of the sentence.

Could such principles possibly constitute a semantic theory in the traditional sense—a theory whose purpose is to provide a semantic interpretation for each sentence of the language? Is it even analogous to one?

A theory of this sort would seem, prima facie, to be a poor candidate, since the translation algorithms that mediate between the input sentences and their representations in the interlingual mode do not constitute a semantic theory. As I suggest in the following paragraphs, the translation process relies on a semantic theory, but one provided by the natural language itself. Since the translation algorithm alone specifies neither truth conditions nor word references, it is difficult, at best, to construe it as a bona fide theory of meaning. It might, however, be construed as analogous to one in the following sense. Consider once again the sentence *John hit Mary* and how that sentence is provided with its appropriate reference within the machine. Suppose two consecutive sentences were read into the machine: *John hit Mary* and *He was angry*. Unless *John* and the pronoun *he* referred to the same person, the two sentences could be construed to be about two different people. In order to understand the connection between John's anger and John hitting Mary, the semantic interpretation of *John* and the referent of *he* would have to be the same. Establishing the referent of *John* would have to occur for the appropriate connection to be made; can establishing the referent of *John* be understood as a classical semantic interpretation? A proper answer to this question requires describing the semantic resources of both program and machine. Do they really have any? We need an account, for example, of how this connection, this process of semantic interpretation, between the proper name *John* and its referent might be established.

It has been suggested that the compiler might be the proper vehicle for providing a semantic interpretation. Once the program is compiled, semantic interpretation would then be tantamount to translating sentences in a step-by-step manner into the language of the machine. Only in this sense, could it be argued that the compiler provides the semantic interpretation by providing the translation from the programming language, such as LISP, into the machine language. Is such a proposal realistic? In what sense can we say that translation into the machine language provides an interpretation genuinely analogous to a classical interpretation?

Consider for a moment the very nature and purpose of the machine language. Understood literally, the power of the digital computer to perform operations resides in its electronic circuitry. In order to direct the operations of that circuitry, a rule-governed command language is required—a language that controls the distribution of electricity through the circuitry of the machine. This language must be one that the machine can process. Euphemistically speaking, this language could be called the language of the silicon chips, since the symbols of that language govern the machine's operations. With this in mind, we ask if the language of the silicon chips or, more accurately, the language used to direct the electronic states and processes of the machine is semantically interpreted. Are its symbols genuinely about things and people?

If the machine language is about anything at all, it is the electronic states of its circuitry. Technically, however, we cannot even say this, since the machine's code directing the flow of current is a command language, and not a descriptive language; it commands the machine: Do *X*, do *Y* or if *X*, do *Y*. At best, expressions of the machine language, written in the two-digit alphabet 0 and 1, refer to, or are about, the computer's internal storage devices—its registers and addresses. The semantics of the proper name *John* is restricted to information about that individual that appears at a particular address. The name *John* does not refer to John. Strictly speaking, this is not a semantics at all, since the name tokens that such proper names as *John* receive simply function as formal tokens not as names naming something or someone. Consider, for example, the sentence in the SAM program, *Sunday morning Enver Hoxha, the Premier of Albania, and Mrs. Hoxha arrived in Peking at the invitation of Communist China*. This sentence is translated into machine language by way of the following representation:

((ACTOR TMP32 <=> (★PTRANS★) OBJECT TMP32 TO (★INSIDE★ PART (POLITY POLTYPE (★MUNIC★) POL-NAME (PEKING)))

Notice that the proper name *Enver Hoxha* receives the formal token number TMP32, which refers to information on Enver Hoxha; information to the effect that Hoxha is a person, a male, a premier, and so on. The token does not refer to Enver Hoxha the man. It is quite obvious, of course, to the programmer or anyone who understands the program that the token TMP32 refers to Enver Hoxha; that it has the full range of referential properties common to any or all proper names in the natural language. This full complement of semantic resources is, however, clearly derived from the natural language.

There may be a temptation to regard the token TMP32 referring to information about Enver Hoxha as having a semantic property. This temptation is short-lived, however, once we realize that information stored there is also stored in formal tokens that are themselves without semantic reference. Consider the sequence of tokens TMP32 = Group Member, Person Gender ★Masc★, and so forth, which is itself uninterpreted unless, of course, we rely on the natural language from which the words were taken. But without this natural semantic base, the tokens have only syntactical and transformational properties, which is tantamount to saying that such tokens function only in the formal mode. A language restricted to the manipulation of tokens according to the formal rules of token transformation is, strictly speaking, not a language at all.

The semantic interpretation of a token is only an alleged interpretation, since, as it stands, formal tokens don't refer to anything beyond themselves; they are not about things in the world. What reference exists is only to more formal tokens and operations that are to be performed on them, which places obvious limitations on the kind of understanding that the machine can be said to have. What provides people with genuine linguistic understanding is the semantic interpretation that provides words and expressions with semantic content. When we hear *John hit Mary*, we know something about what is happening to Mary due to the semantic content of the sentence. This, in turn, is a function of the semantic interpretation of noun phrases and predicates. Learning a language means learning what the words of the language can be used to refer to. There is simply no genuine understanding unless the speaker-hearer realizes that the symbols are representations of things and happenings in the world.

That property of a symbol enabling it to signify or represent things and happenings in the world is sometimes referred to as intentionality. Traditionally, however, intentionality, in its primary use, is not attributed to words but to the speaker-hearer who in learning or using a language takes a word, say, *rainbow* to be about something that is nonlinguistic—a rainbow. The point is, thought, in one or another of its various modes, is about the world, and not words. Words are ordered sequences of physical sounds and, as such, bear no relationship to the world independently of the language user. It is true that words and sentences represent, refer to, or are about things and states of affairs, but this truth gives rise to the mistaken belief that linguistic symbols themselves represent or refer. When learning a language, for example, we take it for granted that such words as *dog* and *rainbow* are about dogs and rainbows. Since this suggests that intentionality is an intrinsic property of words, it is surely not the whole story.

When a certain sequence of sounds, such as *rainbow* has intentionality, that is, is about rainbows or can be used to refer to rainbows by a language community, then it has intentionality derivatively, not intrinsically. *Rainbow* derives its intentionality from the speaker's use of it; properly speaking, then, only the language user exhibits intentionality intrinsically. The ascription of intentionality, however, need not necessarily be restricted to human beings; it is properly applied to those organisms whose mental states of hoping, believing, expecting, fearing, and seeing are directed toward objects or states of affairs whether the latter exist or not. And directing thought toward objects is the property of intentionality. When a person hopes, he hopes for something to happen, whether it does so or not; when he believes, he believes that something is the case, whether it is or not; when he fears, he is fearful of something, whether that something is real or not. In short, mental states have by their very nature a directedness about them that distinguishes them from sequences of physical sound. In this sense, beliefs, desires, hopes, and sightings are about or represent their objects. Where our mental states can, very naturally, be said to be about and represent, physical sounds by themselves cannot. Physical sounds can become words and serve as symbols signifying what is independent of them only derivatively through the action of thought.

Philosophers as diverse as John Searle (1979*a*, 1979*b*) and Roderick Chisholm (1938) have argued convincingly along these lines, contending that the intentionality of words and sentences depends on the psychological states of believing, hoping, wanting, and so forth. The "aboutness" of words and their referential properties presuppose the concept of mental meaning and mental reference, which is not to argue that thinking goes on wholly independently of language but that thoughts are about things and, as a consequence, so are words. As Searle explains, "Language does not create intentionality; rather ... in an important sense intentionality provides the foundation for linguistic acts" (Searle 1979*a*, 190).

Conferring intentionality on physical sounds or marks on paper by the mind is complicated; however, considering the following scenario will help clarify the concepts. You are driving east toward Boston. It is raining, but a break in the clouds lets the sun appear. With the sun low behind you in the west, a rainbow is produced in the east. Pointing to the rainbow, you utter the one-word sentence *rainbow*. In uttering the word *rainbow*, you are making an assertion; properly expanded, it would be *It is a rainbow* or *There is a rainbow*. But what makes the one-word sentence *rainbow* a word that can be used to speak about or refer to the rainbow? Essential to the use of this word for making an assertion is a mental state; in this case, a belief on the part of the speaker that what stretches across the eastern sky is a rainbow. Why is the belief that this is a rainbow necessary for the word *rainbow* to be about rainbows? Briefly, because words are like parasites; they derive their essential properties, in this case, their intentionality, from their hosts. For words, hosts are psychological states that represent their respective objects. My beliefs, hopes, wants, fears represent a world of objects to or for me. These beliefs are not always correct nor are my fears always warranted nor my desires always realized. Nevertheless, it is those psychological states which represent those objects or states of affairs that motivate my actions. My beliefs, whether true or false, represent those objects I pursue or avoid; my fears, when justified, represent some real state of affairs the anticipation of which makes me fearful; my desires, when satisfied, represent the object or person or state of affairs that satisfies them. In short, such psychological states are naturally representational; sequences of sound or marks on paper are not. Thus, the questions remains: How do our mental states, which are naturally or intrinsically representational, confer this same property on sequences of sound, which are not?

Earlier it was suggested that the meaning of a sentence is its truth conditions, and therein lies the bridge from mind to meaning. With the notion of truth conditions in hand, the question can now be rephrased. What role do mental states play in transforming sequences of sound into sentences with truth conditions? A convincing answer to this question follows from Searle's insight that underlying the conversion of sound into sense is the fact that truth conditions for sentences are identical with those of a corresponding belief. Just as the presence of a rainbow is a condition for the truth of my belief, the presence of a rainbow is a condition for the truth of the sentence *There is a rainbow*. The truth condition for the sentence is derived, as it were, from my belief. With this priority in mind, Searle is prompted to say that intentionality is conferred on utterances by transferring to them those conditions of truth that are identical with those for the truth of our psychological states, such as my belief that before me is a rainbow. Searle's way of putting it sounds contrived, but the thrust of his point is convincing, nevertheless. It is unlikely that Searle believes that we first consciously determine the truth conditions of a belief and then transfer those conditions to a sentence. Rather, in asserting with the sentence *There's a rainbow*, my belief that what I see is a rainbow is necessary for making the assertion.

My belief provides the psychological underpinning for making an assertion because unless I believe that what I am looking at is a rainbow, I cannot logically assert that it is one. What provides a sentence with its representational property, its aboutness, is that it satisfies, when true, the same condition that the belief satisfies, namely, that things are as I believe them to be. If there is a satisfactory answer to the question what confers intentionality on language, it must involve those correlative notions of truth and belief. When the conditions that satisfy the psychological state of belief satisfy the truth of the formal token, meaning exists. Only in this manner can mind confer intentionality on formal items that are not themselves intrinsically intentional.

If the thesis that the intentionality of thought is necessary to account for the representational property of words is essentially correct, what are the prospects for developing programs that genuinely simulate human understanding of sentences? Can intentionality or the mechanism that makes intentionality possible be built into the program? Some have suggested that a causal account of semantic interpretation might provide that mechanism; that is, equip the machine with sensory transducers so that sensory information of the right sort is provided for the program. The formal tokens would receive an interpretation by virtue of a causal chain of events connecting them to the sensory information transmitted by the transducers. Such expressions as proper names and predicates could then be used to refer to their respective objects as a consequence of the fact that certain properties of an object are causally related to the expressions themselves. This causal lineage converts the formal token into a genuine symbol with semantic content, which, when used in accordance with the conventions of a speech community, would convey information about the world. So interpreted, linguistic tokens would thereby have the property that anything must have to qualify as a representation: the property of being about *X*, whatever *X* might be, as a consequence of causal connections between *X* and whatever represents it. On providing the formal token *T* with a semantic interpretation construed as a causal chain of events connecting *X* with *T*, *T* could then be used to refer to *X*, name *X*, or describe *X*. That, in outline, is the substance of a causal account of semantic interpretation.

This truncated version of the causal theory of meaning does something less than complete justice to important conceptual distinctions that point to the causal theorist's sensitivity to certain mind-related properties that a system must have to qualify as a system with genuine semantic resources. But even after more careful specification of these distinctions, our questions will be essentially the same: Can machines with causal properties of the sort delineated by the theory exhibit the kind of understanding of sentence meaning that humans have? Does such a theory provide the system (machine plus program) with the kind of causal topography that accounts for the referential use of words? Can a theory that appeals to causal chains connecting word to world provide an adequate account of the intentionality of expressions that qualifies them for referential use?

Take the case of a simple proper name. In order to account for the fact that the name *Elmer Brown* can be used to refer to Elmer Brown, it is not sufficient to point to the capacity of a system to extract information about Elmer Brown from a variety of different sensory signals, even though the information is properly represented in the system as semantic content. All that exists at this point is the token and the semantic content standing idly together; what is it that associates the two, confers the semantic content on the token *for* the system? The basic conventions of naming could not occur except for the fact that these tokens are assumed *by* the system to be about some source of experience. For a name or sentence token to have intentionality, it must be taken as a representation of something *by* the system. Conferring semantic content on a token does not occur in the system by the appropriate causal mechanisms even where those mechanisms transform sensory information into propositional or semantic content.

To assume that the capacity to take something to represent or signify something else can be wholly accounted for in causal terms is unwarranted, since taking something to represent something else cannot itself be the result of a causal process; it is, rather, the beginning of one. Taking *X* to mean or be about *Y* requires an action on the part of an agent where *X* is taken to mean *Y by* or *for* that agent and other members of the speech community. Even if beliefs could be causally produced in a system so that semantic content were properly represented in the system, it would still require a transitive act on the part of an agent for whom the symbol were virtually identical with the thing symbolized—the act of letting *X* be about *Y*. Any system having this capacity has not only the requisite intentionality as a consequence of certain mental states but the capacity of letting physical sounds and marks serve as surrogates for "goings on" in the world. Machines have yet to exhibit this property; causal theories of representation have yet to explain it.

Bibliography

PART I

Boden, Margaret A. *Artificial Intelligence and Natural Man*. New York: Basic Books, 1977.

An excellent introduction to the aims, terminology, and working principles of AI. Boden provides an extensive and clear analysis of the objectives and limitations of a variety of programs ranging from Colby's psychological neurosis program, Abelson's political ideology program, Schank's language comprehension programs, Winograd's block world program to work presently being done in computer vision. The last section is devoted to the psychological, philosophical, and social implications of AI.

Dennett, Daniel. *Content and Consciousness*. London: Routledge and Kegan Paul, 1969.

A technical and philosophical analysis of concepts central to modeling the mind. Dennett focuses on the properties of those systems that can be said to have intentionality and the relationship those properties have to their neurophysiological correlates.

———. *Brainstorms*. Montgomery: Bradford Books, 1969.

A collection of very readable essays on theory of mind first introduced in *Content and Consciousness* (1969). Although each essay is an elaboration of the essential principles of this theory of mind, they vary widely in purpose and subject. Dennett considers the philosophical implications of Godel's theorem; why a computer that feels pain cannot be constructed; AI as philosophy and psychology; issues of free will and personhood; and the nature of sensations, dreams, images, and pains.

Dreyfus, Hubert L. *What Computers Can't Do*. 2nd. ed. New York: Harper and Row, 1972.

An early critique of AI that focuses on differences between the highly abstracted settings within which existing programs operate and those rich human settings that would seem to defy reduction to explicit algorithmic procedures.

Fodor, Jerry A. *The Language of Thought*. New York: Thomas Y. Crowell, 1975.

An essay on speculative psychology, *The Language of Thought* offers a novel approach to modeling such higher cognitive processes as reasoning, concept formation, and perception. Fodor argues that these cognitive abilities are essentially computational processes and consequently require an internal medium of representation in order to be carried out. More controversial, however, is Fodor's contention that learning a natural language requires a system of internal representation at least as semantically rich as the natural language itself. Hence, he concludes that at least some cognitive operations are carried on in languages other than natural languages. This unlearned language of thought, with its own vocabulary and grammar that forms the basis for our higher cognitive operations, is one with which we are innately endowed.

———. "Tom Swift and His Procedural Grandmother." ***Cognition*** **6 (1978): 229–247.**

A humorous but responsible analysis and critique of computational semantics as formulated by P. Johnson-Laird and G. Miller in *Language and Perception* (1976). Some understanding of the aims and methods of classical semantics is helpful.

Haugeland, John, ed. ***Mind Design.*** **Cambridge: MIT Press, 1981.**

A rich collection of twelve articles and a helpful introduction to the objectives of cognitive science by the editor Haugeland. Of the twelve articles, five are written by scientists in the AI field, while the remainder reflect the views of philosophers on subjects ranging from new suggestions on knowledge representation, the properties of intentional systems, the prospects for a materialist theory of mind, and the cognitive capacities of present-day programs. The editor maintains that "mostly, these essays are nontechnical and intended for a wide audience of nonspecialists."

Heil, John. "Does Cognitive Psychology Rest on a Mistake?" ***Mind*** **90 (1981): 321–336.**

A close look by a philosopher at the implications of a computational theory of mind as formulated by Jerry Fodor in *The Language of Thought* (1975). Heil questions the validity of the computational theorist's contention that the internal states of a digital computer may be regarded as representational or symbolic.

Hofstadter, Douglas R., and Daniel C. Dennett, eds. ***The Mind's I.*** **New York: Basic Books, 1981.**

By way of science fiction fantasies, philosophical forays, imaginative dialogues (one with Einstein's brain), the elusive I is pursued by twenty-six thinkers. Subtitled *Fantasies and Reflections on Self and Soul*, these essays probe the limits of possible but credible answers to such questions as: What is the self? What is it that I am? What is it like to be me? What is it like to be a bat? Could a robot or computer be conscious? How can a physical body in a physical world have mental experiences? Can more than one self be in one body? The preface states: "designed to provoke, disturb, and befuddle its readers, to make the obvious strange and, perhaps, to make the strange obvious"—and this collection is eminently successful in its exploration of the possible.

Ringle, Martin, ed. ***Philosophical Perspectives in Artificial Intelligence.*** **Atlantic Highlands, N. J.: Humanities Press, 1979.**

A wide-ranging collection of articles by AI practitioners and philosophers edited by Ringle, who has also contributed a helpful, brief history documenting the changing goals, methodologies, and aspirations of the new science. Examples of recent work in the field are presented by Wendy Lehnert, John McDermott, John McCarthy, and Roger Schank. In the remaining articles, philosophers and psychologists are given the opportunity of assessing the extent to which efforts in AI to model the human mind have been successful.

Schank, Roger C. "Conceptual Dependency: A Theory of Natural Language Understanding." ***Cognitive Psychology*** **3 (1972): 552–631.**

An early statement of Schank's conceptual dependency theory that forms part of a broader theory of human understanding. Schank's thesis is that understanding sentences in a natural language involves mapping the sentences into a conceptual base that is common to all languages. Schank introduces the symbolism that represents some of the concepts available in a natural language.

———. *Conceptual Information Processing*. Amsterdam: North-Holland Publishing, 1975.

An in-depth analysis of a theory of natural-language processing, with a description of various computer programs that implement the theory. The programs described make up the MARGIE system, which makes inferences and paraphrases from natural-language sentences.

———. "How Much Intelligence Is There in Artificial Intelligence?" *Intelligence* 4 (1980): 1–14.

This essay explores the question of machine intelligence from the standpoint of language-comprehension tasks. Schank's thesis is that neither problem solving nor ability to reason are primary indicators of intelligence but rather the ability to use knowledge of the world stored in memory.

Schank, Roger C., and Kenneth M. Colby, eds. *Computer Models of Thought and Language*. San Francisco: W. H. Freeman, 1973.

The unifying theme of this collection is modeling human psychological processes on a computer. All ten articles by experts in the field of AI represent a theoretical commitment to a view of man as a conceptual, intentional, and semantic-based system. The articles deal with the theoretical problems of modeling the role of thought, memory, and belief in the comprehension of language.

Schank, Roger C., and Robert P. Abelson, eds. *Scripts, Plans, Goals, and Understanding*. Hillsdale, N. J.: Laurence Erlbaum, 1977.

Subtitled *An Inquiry into Human Knowledge Structures*; this book documents the ongoing research on how knowledge is stored in memory and brought to bear on understanding sentences in a natural language. Portions of programs using scripts, plans, and goals for the purpose of interpreting sentences are provided.

Searle, John R. "What Is an Intentional State?" *Mind* 88 (1979): 72–94.

———. "Intentionality and the Use of Language." In *Meaning and Use*, edited by A. Margalit. Hingham, Mass., and The Hague: Reidel, 1979.

Both articles provide technical and philosophical analyses of the intentionality of mental states and the essential role these states play in linguistic representation.

———. "Minds, Brains, and Programs." *The Behavioral and Brain Sciences* 3 (1980): 417–424.

In this much anthologized essay, Searle focuses on the shortcomings of extant language-comprehension programs. Searle's imaginative Chinese-language thought experiment points out the cognitive limitations of a system restricted to the formal manipulation of symbols.

Weizenbaum, Joseph. *Computer Power and Human Reason*. San Francisco: W. H. Freeman, 1976.

Perhaps the most helpful introduction to the theoretical principles underlying the power of the computer to reason and think. Weizenbaum guides the reader through the conceptual underpinnings of the Turing machine, Church's thesis, the notion of an effective procedure, and formal transformation rules. After providing the reader with a sense of what makes the computer the kind of "thinker" it is, Weizenbaum addresses the philosophical issue of whether computers understand—think—in the same way that humans do.

Alfeld, Louis E., and Alan K. Graham. *Introduction to Urban Dynamics*. Cambridge: MIT Press, 1976.

Organized as a textbook with practical exercises at the end of each chapter, this book explains the interactions behind the growth of a city by using simulation models. Sequential evolution of ten urban models presents the assumptions, structure, behavior, and utility of urban dynamic models for urban policy analysis. These models are based on Forrester's *Urban Dynamics*, but the ideas behind Forrester's work are presented in a simpler manner than in the original book.

Andersen, David F., and George P. Richardson. "A Core Curriculum in System Dynamics." Occasional Paper GSPA 1–79, Graduate School of Public Affairs, State University of New York at Albany, 1979.

This paper discusses ideas and concepts that a system dynamics curriculum should emphasize. An extensive bibliography lists useful curriculum materials.

Burnham, David. *Rise of the Computer State*. New York: Random House, 1983.

A new analysis by a *New York Times* reporter that focuses on the societal impact of computers, emphasizing dangers and negative consequences. The effects on representative government are illustrated by many examples. Sections focus on data bases, political power, surveillance, and intelligence. A general discussion of the future and the roles of various interest groups is included.

Coyle, R. G. *Management System Dynamics*. London: Wiley, 1977.

This book deals with the design of managerial policies that will help an organization perform satisfactorily over time in the face of external shocks and under the influence of internal processes. The book covers specific techniques for modeling corporate problems, analysing the results, and redesigning corporate policies to improve behavior. The book includes several examples drawn from projects performed by the author and his associates.

Dertouzos, M., and J. Moses. *The Computer Age: A Twenty-Year View*. Cambridge: MIT Press, 1980.

An edited series of papers that gives an excellent overview of applications of computers; trends in their use and trends in underlying and related technologies; and social effects and expectations. Individual papers deal with world affairs (Gilpin), modeling (Shubik), and critiques of computer development (Weizenbaum and responders: Bell and Dertouzos). The Gilpin paper discusses computers in military affairs but largely in weapons development.

Dorsen, Norman, and Stephen Grilers, eds. *None of your Business: Government Secrecy in America*. New York: Viking, 1974.

Informative collection of essays addressing the relationship between government secrecy and the right of citizens to have access to information. The perspective of the readings is that the relationship is adversarial; therefore, the analysis stresses how government secrecy, as a means of power, jeopardizes democracy, while, at the same time, exploring protective recourses available to citizens.

***Dynamica*. System Dynamics Research Group, University of Bradford, Bradford, U. K. BD7 1DP.**

A quarterly journal publishing research papers in system dynamics.

Flaherty, David H. *Privacy and Government Data Banks: An International Perspective*. London: Mansell, 1979.

An investigation of the uses of government data in modern industrially advanced societies. This book represents a cross-national study of the problems of privacy and confidentiality created when governmental research and statistical agencies aggregate and disseminate data in the United Kingdom, Sweden, the Federal Republic of Germany, the United States, and Canada. Each country is systematically discussed and compared. Particularly meritorious is Flaherty's chapter presenting his conclusions and recommendations based on the general finding that the menace posed by the data imperative is largely exaggerated.

Forrester, Jay W. *Industrial Dynamics*. Cambridge: MIT Press, 1961.

This first complete presentation of the system dynamics approach to the study of industrial systems explains objectives, testing model validity, and application of system dynamics to industrial problems. Several appendices contain technical information about system dynamics found nowhere else.

———. *Principles of Systems*. Cambridge: MIT Press, 1968.

This is the introductory text on system dynamics. It introduces the basic concepts of system structure, then shows by example how structure determines behavior. The book contains ten chapters of text followed by workbook problems and answers. Although the problems are framed in a corporate context, the principles are applicable to many fields. The book assumes that the reader knows algebra but does not depend on prior knowledge of calculus. It is suitable for use at the high school and college levels.

———. *World Dynamics*. Cambridge: MIT Press, 1973.

Describing the work that preceeded *Limits to Growth*, this book explains a world model that quantifies interrelationships among population, food production, capital investment, natural resources, pollution, and the quality of life. The book describes this model (of about forty-five DYNAMO equations) equation by equation and discusses general results obtained from the model. This model is useful as an example of system dynamics and simple enough to be run and modified by students without extensive time spent on learning its structure.

———. *Collected Papers of Jay W. Forrester*. Cambridge: MIT Press, 1975.

This book describes a range of applications of system dynamics from early industrial examples to extensions to urban and national economic-policy design. Included in this collection of seventeen of Forrester's papers is his testimony before the House of Representatives Subcommittee on Urban Growth and addresses before the National Council of Churches and the National Academy of Engineering.

Goodman, Michael R. *Study Notes in System Dynamics*. Cambridge: MIT Press, 1974.

A basic text in system dynamics that is especially useful in conjuction with *Principles of Systems*, but is not complete enough to be used alone as an introduction to the field. Part 1 focuses on simple structures and describes elements of positive and negative feedback loops. Part 2 reinforces material in the first part with eight exercises emphasizing the relationship between structure and behavior. Part 3 contains advanced exercises on model conceptualization and analysis.

Hiltz, Roxanne S., and Murray Turoff . *The Network Nation*. Reading, Mass.: Addison-Wesley, 1978.

This book resulted from the development of a new communications technology known as computer conferencing. Much of the knowledge about conferencing was acquired by observing the use of the electronic information exchange system (EIES) developed by Murray Turoff, one of the authors. The book discusses various applications and results of a computer conferencing system.

Hoffman, Lance. *Computers and Privacy in the Next Decade*. New York: Academic Press, 1980.

Collection of articles first presented to the American Federation of Information Processing Societies analyzing the long-term impact of changing information technology and the protection of personal privacy. Areas on the research agenda are identified and alternative research strategies and methods are evaluated.

Hoos, Ida R. *Systems Analysis in Public Policy: A Critique*. Berkeley and Los Angeles: University of California Press, 1972.

Excellent skeptical and rigorous overview of use of systems approach in a variety of public policy areas. Theoretical and practical issues, with a final session devoted to "futurology". Many of the problems of systems analysis are highlighted.

Hopewell, Lynn et al. *Proceedings of the Federal Communications Planning Conference November 8 and 9, 1976*. Montvale, N. J.: AFIPS Press, 1976.

This is an accumulation of technical presentations given at the request of the FCC to address computer and communications technologies. It was part of the FCC's computer inquiry to reexamine interrelationships of computer and communications technology.

Landon, Kenneth C. *Computers and Bureaucratic Reform: The Political Functions of Urban Information Systems*. New York: Wiley, 1974.

The author examines how progressive values are to be maintained when confronted by counteracting forces unleashed in the modern technological period. He argues that administrative overcentralization and inertial consequents are not inherent technological requisites, but products of calculated political decisions. Why the bureaucratic use of computer information systems increases the likelihood of static social policy outputs is extensively discussed through case studies of health, police, and welfare programs. The concluding chapter includes a discussion of how dynamics of the political system can be employed to remedy these developments.

Levin, Gilbert, and Edward B. Roberts. *The Dynamics of Human-Service Delivery*. Cambridge, Mass.: Ballinger, 1976.

This book presents several models of factors affecting the delivery of such human services as dental, mental health, and educational services. Chapter 7 describes Roberts's model of factors affecting student performance in the classroom. This model can easily be entered on a computer and simulated using DYNAMO.

Levin, Gilbert, Edward B. Roberts, and Gary Hirsch. *The Persistent Poppy: A Computer-Aided Search for Heroin Policy*. Cambridge, Mass.: Ballinger, 1975.

This book describes the application of system dynamics to the development of government policies on heroin addiction. Sections of the model presented in the book depict the growth of heroin addict populations, the effects of police enforcement, and the impact on the community.

Lighthill, M. J. et al. *Telecommunications in the 1980s and after*. Cambridge: Cambridge University Press, 1978.

This book is a composite of papers given at a Royal Society meeting held in 1977 to discuss future patterns of telecommunication development. These papers cover all aspects of modern telecommunications from technology to its implications.

Margulis, Stephen T., issue ed. "Privacy as a Behavior Phenomenon." *Journal of Social Issues* 33, no. 3 (1977).

This issue contains eleven articles on privacy in society from a behavioral perspective. These articles generally stress an applied socio-psychological perspective and are built on hypotheses and concepts from literature examining the social dimensions of privacy in a political and historical framework. The collection of articles illustrates how the behavioral approach can span the gaps between various disciplines concerned with privacy.

Martin, James T. *Future Developments in Telecommunications*. Englewood Cliffs, N. J.: Prentice-Hall, 1977.

Martin is known internationally for his books on communications and data base. In this book, he introduces the changing technology of communications and highlights the rapidity with which this change is taking place and proves himself to be a very good forecaster of things to come.

———. *The Wired Society*. Englewood Cliffs, N. J.: Prentice-Hall, 1978.

This book was nominated for a Pulitzer Prize. It is written in lay terms and projects the "rewiring of America," describing scenarios of the impacts that changes will have on the future quality of life.

Martin, J., and A. R. D. Norman. *The Computerized Society*. Englewood Cliffs, N. J.: Prentice-Hall, 1970.

A general treatment of the applications of computers and the issues they raise. One section is devoted to a range of problem areas, including the relationship of computers to political power, and another to possible ways of dealing with those problems.

Martino, Joseph P. *The Digital Impact—Transmission, Switching*. Cambridge: The Yankee Group, 1979.

This book addresses the impact of digital technology on equipment currently employed in the field of communications. The equipment it discusses falls into the categories of transmission, switching, and customer-premise equipment. Although it stresses equipment-market opportunities, the book reviews the overall equipment market.

———. "Pathways to the Information Society." *Proceedings of the Sixth International Conference on Computer Communications London 7–10 September 1982*. New York: North-Holland Publishing, 1982.

An accumulation of papers that describe facets of communications from technology to specific applications. A very broad coverage of techindustry. This book contains well over a hundred papers on various subjects related to communications.

———. *Technological Forecasting for Decision Making*. New York: North-Holland Publishing, 1983.

This is a how-to book discussing how to view technological changes and project them into the future. It describes the essential set of tools required by any forecaster and any futurist.

Mass, Nathaniel J. *Economic Cycles: An Analysis of Underlying Causes*. Cambridge: MIT Press, 1975.

This book suggests that labor hiring and termination policies underlie the short-term business cycle, while capital investment policies are primarily involved in generating economic cycles of much longer duration. By providing an understanding of the generic causes of business cycles, the book provides a basis for future investigation of alternative economic-stabilization policies. The book describes in detail a simulation model that provides an example of system dynamics applied to economics.

Meadows, Dennis L., and Donella H. Meadows. *Toward Global Equilibrium: Collected Papers*. Cambridge: MIT Press, 1973.

A collection of studies identifying and treating specific issues connected with *Limits to Growth*. The book contains several small DYNAMO models that can easily be entered into a computer and run with a DYNAMO compiler.

Meadows, Donella H. et al. *The Limits to Growth*. New York: Universe Books, 1972.

This well-known book (over three million copies sold) offers a nontechnical discussion of problems associated with growth in world population and industrial output. The book can be read and understood without any knowledge of system dynamics. It can be used for stimulating discussion about possible futures and economic and population policies.

Meadows, Donella H., John Richardson, and Gerhardt Bruckmann, eds. *Groping in the Dark: The First Decade of Global Modelling*. New York: Wiley, 1982.

A guide to the successes and failures of global modeling since the publication of *The Limits to Growth* ten years ago. The text is based on the sixth symposium of the International Institute for Applied Systems Analysis. Since the Forrester/Meadows model was published, a number of models have emerged; the intention in each case was to improve the model sufficiently in order to avoid some of the criticisms aimed at the original. The difficulties of global modeling are immense—not the least of which is their inadequacy with respect to the nature and strength of political and social variables.

Petrocelli, William. *Low Profile: How to Avoid the Privacy Invaders*. New York: McGraw Hill, 1981.

An anecdotal but highly engaging discussion of dangers posed by the privacy invaders to the principles of individualism and liberty; spiced with factual illustrations, quotes, and personal interest stories. Petrocelli explores complex problems arising from the insatiably acquisitive drive in a postindustrial society for information and recommends ways that individuals can protect themselves from the loss of privacy.

Privacy Protection Study Commission. *Personal Privacy in an Information Society*. Washington, D. C., July 1977.

Established by the Privacy Act of 1974, this commission examined the required balance between personal privacy needs and legitimate informational demands by public and private sector agencies. This report is the outcome of that investigation and, as such, a comprehensive review of general and specific questions on striking the proper balance in order to guide national policy. Private sector record-keeping, concerns involving consumer credit agencies, bank depository institutions, direct mailing firms, insurance organizations, and medical care facilities receive extensive and informative treatment. Education, public assistance and social services, taxes, social security, and general research and development are areas of public policy addressed by the report.

Pugh, Alexander L. *DYNAMO User's Manual*. Cambridge: MIT Press, 1976.

This book provides a complete description of DYNAMO, including the advanced forms of the language—DYNAMO II and DYNAMO III.

Pylyshyn, Z. W. *Perspectives on the Computer Revolution*. Englewood Cliffs, N. J.: Prentice-Hall, 1970.

An edited collection of papers on the implication of computers that tends to focus on more psychological and philosophical aspects while still providing down-to-earth information. As a result, it is somewhat less policy oriented than other analyses but raises some profound social issues.

Roberts, Edward B. *Managerial Applications of System Dynamics*. Cambridge: MIT Press, 1978.

This text is currently used in the M.I.T. Sloan School's regular graduate programs and middle-management executive-development programs. It documents approximately forty applications of system dynamics in business. The first chapter is a concise explanation of the fundamental concepts of system dynamics and DYNAMO. Each part of the book begins with an overview containing references to related applications not included in the book as well as to some applications that are not documented at all in the literature.

Roberts, Nancy. *Dynamic Feedback Systems Kit*. Cambridge, Mass.: Pugh-Roberts, 1979.

This booklet provides materials used in teaching feedback concepts to elementary school children. The booklet contains four parts: a discussion of how to use the material, a set of exercises involving an explanation of causal-loop diagrams, a set of stories from which causal-loop diagrams are constructed, and suggested solutions to the stories.

Robertson, A. H., ed. *Privacy and Human Rights*. Manchester, U. K.: Manchester University Press, 1973.

The essays in this volume are based on discussions at one of a continuing series of international conferences examining the impact of the European Convention on Human Rights on the protection of individual and family privacy. Approaches taken in these essays reflect the juridical perspective of the convention's provisions for privacy in a modern technological age.

Rule, James et al. *The Politics of Privacy*. New York: Mentor Book, 1980.

An outgrowth of a report submitted to a Study Commission on Privacy Protection, this book examines how expanded government record-keeping needs and societal use of computerization technology threaten the fundamental right of individual privacy. The limits of national planning and procedural safeguards aimed at balancing the tension between the government's need to know and personal liberties are discussed.

Shaffer, William A. *Mini-DYNAMO User's Guide*. Cambridge, Mass.: Pugh-Roberts, 1978.

This guide explains in detail the operation of the Mini-DYNAMO system and control statements in DYNAMO. It can be used as a companion to *Principles of Systems* to provide an introduction to DYNAMO.

Simulation. *Society for Computer Simulation*, P. O. Box 2228, La Jolla, Calif. 92037.

Smith, Robert E. *Privacy: How to Protect What's Left of It?* New York: Anchor Press/Doubleday, 1979.

Smith tries to document the pervasive invasion of personal privacy in the modern age. A broad discussion of the new technology from computer to electronic surveillance devices is presented to support the argument. A description of the intrusive impact of this technology includes the informational, physical, and psychological dimensions. How the public and private sectors obtain information on citizens is a major feature of the first part of the discussion.

***System Dynamics Newsletter*, System Dynamics Group, E40–253, MIT, Cambridge, Mass. 02139.**

An annual compendium of activities in the field of system dynamics, including both educational and research activities. It contains a cumulative bibliography of most of the books and papers published in system dynamics.

U. S. Congress. Office of Technology Assessment. *Computer-Based National Information System: Technology and Public Policy Issues*. 1981.

The publication assays the impact of computer and communication technology on a number of different public policy issues. Included are questions of innovation, productivity and employment, privacy, security, governmental management of data processing, constitutional rights, boundaries of regulatory policy, and technological safeguards against system failures. A very good summary chapter presents a quick overview of the book.

U.S. Congress. Senate. Committee on Government Operations. Inquiry of the Subcommittee on National Security and International Operations. *Planning, Programming, Budgeting*. March 1970.

Particularly interesting testimony and papers on the use of systems analysis techniques in foreign affairs and national security. Testimony by Thomas Schelling ("PPBS and Foreign Affairs"), James R. Schlesinger ("Uses and Abuses of Analysis"), Frederick Mosher ("Program Budgeting in Foreign Affairs"), Alain Enthoven ("Systems Analysis"), Aaron Wildavsky ("Rescuing Policy Analysis from PPBS"), and others.

Westin, Alan F. *Privacy and Freedom*. New York: Atheneum, 1967.

A comprehensive but highly readable study of the central question faced by societies experiencing the modern technological revolution—How can the knowledge explosion be harnessed to best serve the interests of democratic liberties and individual privacy? Five case studies examining the consequences of the rapidly expanding use of sophisticated surveillance devices highlight the discussion of the political and social struggle with this issue in America.

Westin, A. F., ed. *Information Technology in a Democracy*. Cambridge: Harvard University Press, 1971.

An edited series of excellent papers from highly qualified authors, touching on many of the issues associated with computers, including those issues raised for society. Although most of the papers deal with largely domestic issues, several (Enthoven, Schelling, and Schlesinger) are concerned with military and international affairs. In any case, many of the pieces have civilian or military applications. While over a decade old, this volume continues to raise pertinent issues.

Westin, Alan F., and Michael Baker. *Databanks in a Free Society*. New York: Quadrangle Books, 1972.

A far-ranging study of impact of data processing, storage, and communications questions in various governmental, commercial, and private organizations. Extensive observations on organizational record-keeping procedures and civil-liberty protection mechanisms are documented and evaluated. Particularly interesting is the discussion on accuracy and security problems created by faulty or contradictory procedures. Westin and associates try to forecast the possible direction of emerging and continually changing computer technology and discuss public policy ramifications of some of these developments. Readers who feel comfortable with hard data and statistics will find the material in each of the three appendices most valuable.

Wheeler, Stanton. *On Record: Files and Dossiers in American Life*. New York: Russell Sage, 1969.

A compilation of fourteen papers concentrating on descriptive accounts of record use in different organizations. By exploring the conditions under which different types of records are kept, the social functions of record keeping, and the social and legal consequences of record keeping on individuals and organizations, the authors hope to generate specific propositions that will lead to a better understanding of the general function in, and effect of file maintenance on, the American society. Studies of educational, military, economic, and governmental agencies highlight the analysis presented here.